Vertical Gardening

A Beginner's Guide to Growing Fruit, Vegetables, Herbs and Flowers on a Living Wall and How to Create an Urban Garden in Small Spaces

© Copyright 2021

The content contained within this book may not be reproduced, duplicated, or transmitted without direct written permission from the author or the publisher.

Under no circumstances will any blame or legal responsibility be held against the publisher, or author, for any damages, reparation, or monetary loss due to the information contained within this book, either directly or indirectly.

Legal Notice:

This book is copyright protected. It is only for personal use. You cannot amend, distribute, sell, use, quote, or paraphrase any part of the content within this book without the consent of the author or publisher.

Disclaimer Notice:

Please note the information contained within this document is for educational and entertainment purposes only. All effort has been executed to present accurate, up-to-date, reliable, complete information. No warranties of any kind are declared or implied. Readers acknowledge that the author is not engaging in the rendering of legal, financial, medical, or professional advice. The content within this book has been derived from various sources. Please consult a licensed professional before attempting any techniques outlined in this book.

By reading this document, the reader agrees that under no circumstances is the author responsible for any losses, direct or indirect, that are incurred as a result of the use of the information contained within this document, including, but not limited to, errors, omissions, or inaccuracies.

Table of Contents

INTRODUCTION..1
CHAPTER 1: THE BENEFITS OF VERTICAL GARDENS AND
LIVING WALLS..3
    WHY ARE VERTICAL GARDENS BENEFICIAL? 5
    PLACING YOUR NEW VERTICAL GARDEN..6
    VERTICAL GARDENS ARE TRENDY! 9
    WHY CHOOSE A VERTICAL GARDEN? 10
CHAPTER 2: WHERE TO PLACE YOUR VERTICAL GARDEN 12
    KEEPING YOUR LIVING WALLS ALIVE..16
    WHAT TYPE OF PLANTS SHOULD YOU CHOOSE? 17
    SUNLIGHT VS. SHADE..18
CHAPTER 3: PICKING THE RIGHT SOIL..20
    SOIL TYPES..20
    WHAT NUTRIENTS DO PLANTS NEED? 25
    ADDING NUTRIENTS TO YOUR SOIL (ORGANICALLY)...................26
    HOW MUCH SOIL DO YOU NEED? 27
    THINGS TO CONSIDER WHEN PREPARING FOR A VERTICAL
    GARDEN 28
CHAPTER 4: CONTAINERS, PLANTERS, AND TRELLISES........................30
    DIYS: MAKING YOUR OWN CONTAINERS, PLANTERS, AND
    TRELLISES..35
CHAPTER 5: THE VERTICAL GARDENING START-UP 40
    INSTALLING YOUR FIRST VERTICAL GARDEN 41

DIYING A DRIP IRRIGATION SYSTEM 47
CHAPTER 6: BEST PLANTS FOR YOUR VERTICAL GARDEN 49
    THE BEST PLANTS FOR LIVING WALLS 65
CHAPTER 7: FRUIT TREES FOR YOUR VERTICAL GARDEN 75
CHAPTER 8: VERTICAL VEGGIES 92
CHAPTER 9: GROWING FLOWERS ON A LIVING WALL............................. 106
CHAPTER 10: CONTROLLING WEEDS, DISEASES, AND PESTS................. 118
    WATERING NEEDS 120
    SUNLIGHT VS. SHADE.. 121
    IMBALANCED SOIL... 121
    PESTS AND PLANT DISEASES.. 122
CHAPTER 11: YOUR VERTICAL GARDENING CHECKLIST 126
    STEPS TO TAKE FOR YOUR VERTICAL GARDEN OR LIVING WALL.. 127
CHAPTER 12: FINAL PRECAUTIONS AND CONSIDERATIONS 132
    PROS AND CONS TO CONSIDER 133
CONCLUSION 140
HERE'S ANOTHER BOOK BY DION ROSSER THAT YOU MIGHT LIKE 141
REFERENCES 142

Introduction

This book will introduce you to the world of vertical gardening and living walls, preparing you to take on the exciting challenge of creating your very own. You'll learn what vertical gardening is, how to start and maintain your own garden, and how to ensure a successful experience on your new ecologically friendly journey.

Not only is this book easy to read, but it's also full of the latest information on the subject and a hands-on approach that will help guide you from the very first step. Each chapter will take you through a simple step-by-step approach, teaching you everything you will need to learn before taking off on your own. Each chapter includes instructions on achieving certain tasks and will guide you towards making the right decision for you and your new lifestyle.

Gardening has its challenges, but vertical gardening has a few advantages that may help first-time gardeners, making it the perfect gardening method to start with. You may simply prefer this form of gardening because of a lack of space, but you will soon learn about all it has to offer.

This is vertical gardening 101 and is perfect for those who have no prior knowledge and want to learn about everything, starting with the simplest details.

This is a beginner's guide to growing fruit, vegetables, herbs, or flowers on a living wall or vertical garden, and it will teach you everything you need to know. Besides instructions, you will also find simple DIY tutorials that you can tackle for a more cost-effective take on this project. This book is for every type of beginner.

Chapter 1: The Benefits of Vertical Gardens and Living Walls

As the world has been forced to deal with new and unprecedented circumstances, more and more people are finding themselves working from home. Many of those people have picked up an array of new hobbies, one of which is gardening. Creative people have found solutions to make life easier in every area of our daily lives, so why not explore some modern gardening methods? You've likely heard by now about vertical storage, where storage units are built against walls in every (previously unused) corner of our homes. They're not just space savers; they're also aesthetically pleasing.

Vertical gardens and living walls are the next best thing in gardening; they're the new "vertical storage." Soon, more and more people will adopt this new method. Liberating more space on your countertops, desks, floors, or even balcony and terrace should be on your to-do list. And if you don't do it for the aesthetics, do it for the practicality of these beautiful, living, green walls.

Imagine enjoying a glass of wine or a meal with friends or family while surrounded by a luscious canopy of greenery. Who needs a new lick of paint when you can have the different textures, colors, and scents of a garden envelop you in your very own indoor oasis? An oasis that you grew yourself!

What are Vertical Gardens and Living Walls?

To put it simply, vertical gardens or living walls are exactly what they sound like. They are gardens that can cover entire walls, unlike the typical horizontal gardens we're accustomed to. Vertical gardens are also known as living walls because the plants are real living organisms. You might have even heard of moss walls; moss is a plant commonly used to create living walls.

These gardens may be entirely hydroponic, which is the method of growing plants in nutrient-rich water rather than earth.

These gardens can be as small or as large as you want, and they can contain anything from plants to flowers or even fruit and vegetables. What they all have in common is that they are vertical structures, mostly green, and are sure to add a unique and practical twist to your space. Besides making a great décor statement, they're also incredibly beneficial for different reasons. Find out below why they are beneficial to your home, your health, and more.

Andriez777, CC BY-SA 4.0 <https://creativecommons.org/licenses/by-sa/4.0>, via Wikimedia Commons https://commons.wikimedia.org/wiki/File:Vertical-Garden-Surabaya.jpg

Why are Vertical Gardens Beneficial?

There are plenty of benefits to growing a vertical garden or living wall, and some of them might surprise you.

Take Up Less Space

One of the most obvious advantages to vertical growing is space. You don't need as much space to grow plants, and therefore you can grow even more than you would in a horizontal garden. You can take advantage of even the smallest outdoor areas in your home by growing your own vegetables or herbs with the simple use of a vertical garden. You can also have a raised garden in non-traditional areas like a balcony or on a wall inside your home.

You Don't Need a Green Thumb

While you'll still need to take care of your living wall garden, vertical gardens' upkeep is less taxing than traditional ones. Because they're vertical, common problems that plague traditional gardens like weeds and pests won't be as much of a problem. In fact, soil-borne diseases won't be a problem at all in a hydroponic setup. So, even if you don't feel very confident growing plants, this can be an easier start for you. They still require some maintenance, though, which we will discuss further along in the book.

Easier Harvesting

If you're anything like me, the idea of squatting in a garden for hours looking for bugs and harvesting crops does not excite you. This is another benefit to growing a vertical garden, as there is no need to add strain to your body when collecting the vegetables or herbs you've grown. This is because most of your crops will be at hip-to-shoulder level. This allows even elderly people to create their own garden and grow produce without any help from others.

Reduce Noise

Vertical gardens act as a sound barrier and reduce noise coming into your space from the outside. They can even be more effective than traditional construction materials used to soundproof space. This is why they are sometimes used in offices located in busy streets or apartments facing an avenue with a lot of traffic.

Reduce Temperature

Besides acting as a great soundproofing barrier, living walls also do wonders for areas with high temperatures. Plants lower the temperature of the space around them through a process called transpiration. This process works even during the highest temperature peaks. Imagine a cosmopolitan city with skyscrapers and busy streets; the heat in such places gets trapped between buildings, and even pedestrians can feel the effect. That same city carpeted in beautiful green walls would have an entirely different effect as these living walls would help lower the temperature by a considerable degree. Growing living walls in such places can prove beneficial, especially in years to come, as climate change becomes more of an issue.

Promote Biodiversity

Having plants and flowers around helps preserve ecosystems, and these living walls are no exception. You'll be promoting biodiversity in your area, allowing bees and other beneficial insects to thrive locally. Some living walls installed on buildings even include habitat boxes so that insects and small animals have shelter within those walls.

Placing Your New Vertical Garden

Vertical gardens or living walls are a great addition to dwellings such as townhouses, apartments, office spaces, building facades, hospitals, and more. To onlookers, they are visually appealing, of course, but we also know that they serve several ecological and health purposes.

Townhouses

One benefit of growing a vertical garden in a townhouse is that it's an attractive way to conceal your patio area or a backyard from your next-door neighbors. A freestanding vertical garden helps add some privacy to your outdoor space while also keeping the area looking fresher and quieter. This is especially beneficial during the summers or if you live near busy streets.

Apartments

If you live in an apartment, having your own vertical garden can help bring the outside in, make your space feel cozier, and improve air quality, especially if you live in a big city. Also, if you have a small balcony, you can still grow your own produce because vertical gardens don't take up much floor space. This will allow you to make the most of your balcony's space and turn it into your very own green oasis.

Office Spaces/Workspace

A living wall can guarantee happier, more productive employees and better air quality in an office space. Since plants reduce temperatures, companies will spend less on air-conditioning during the warmer months, thereby reducing energy costs. Moreover, by having an attractive and more relaxing environment, your office will catch clients' attention, which will lead to more business.

Building Facades

If you're considering building a large-scale vertical garden, a full-scale building facade is one way to go. Because vertical gardens are living things, no two green facades will look the same. This means your building will have its own truly unique look. Carpeted by the beauty of this natural facade, your building is sure to stand out and draw positive attention from every onlooker. Of course, the other benefits mentioned above apply here as well; the façade will help lower the temperature in the surrounding area, produce oxygen, and improve people's moods.

https://pixabay.com/es/photos/expo-mil%C3%A1n-jard%C3%ADn-vertical-1157790/

Hospitals

Another possible location for living walls, and perhaps the most surprising one of all, is hospitals. Studies in the International Journal of Environmental Research and Public Health have shown that being surrounded by a calming green environment helps patients recover faster and increases their pain tolerance. You may experience the same soothing effect when out in nature, whether it be a hike in the woods or a picnic near a lake or waterfall. The natural elements contribute to stress relief and healing. This is why living walls are a great addition to hospital wards, especially ones that cater to patients with chronic illnesses.

The idea behind the living walls in all of the places previously mentioned is that they can improve your quality of life through their beauty or practicality. Due to their adaptable size, you can even set up your vertical garden in your bathroom, provided that there's a window. Regardless of where you choose to build it, a vertical garden is sure to be a unique design idea for your home or space.

Vertical Gardens Are Trendy!

If you're still not convinced, telling you vertical gardens or living walls are very "in" right now might just do the trick. There are many reasons why vertical gardens are trendy at the moment, but I'll name a few for you.

Wow-Factor

First and foremost, they're unexpected. People don't expect to find a tall wall of green vegetation indoors. They offer that wow factor that many people love. A hotel lobby or office won't usually have a living wall, but when they do, you're surprised and happy to see them. The living wall makes you feel welcome and instantly more relaxed. Even outside a building, looking up to see a fun, green facade instead of a blank expanse of concrete block is also unexpected. Imagine New York City, a concrete jungle, with new and improved buildings carpeted in beautiful shades of green. It wouldn't be just unexpected and relaxing; it would be breathtaking. Living walls make the urban greys come to life.

Indoor-Outdoor Flow

In your own home, vertical gardens can bring a touch of the outdoors to your indoor space. For those living in small apartments without outside space, like a balcony, having a vertical garden inside your home brings in the aura of life you can find only outside. Plants create a peaceful atmosphere which, especially nowadays, many of us crave. Growing a vertical garden indoors will help you feel like you're outdoors even when you can't go outside.

An Art Form

They offer an easy way to cover up bland, white walls. If you don't want to just hang up another painting on your wall, but you hate blank spaces, it's a creative and fun way to level up your space. A white wall can feel cold and uninviting, whether inside or outside. But, coming up with solutions to make it feel and look more welcoming isn't always straightforward. A living wall can quickly fix that for you.

Aside from covering a blank space, they are considered art. They're not so common that everyone will have seen them before, and they really make a statement. Imagine all the different textures and plants you can add, all the different shapes and sizes; it'll be something to look at and admire. Your guests will be talking about it for days.

For Privacy

If making a statement is not your goal, you may consider this an easy yet beautiful way to add privacy to your home. Unfortunately, as societies grow, we have less space; therefore, our neighbors are getting closer and closer to our private spaces. Sometimes, we need a little help to cover our balcony from the direct view of our neighbors, whether we live in apartments or stand-alone houses. Again, vertical gardens come to the rescue – they create a privacy screen, and because many plants thrive on them, they'll grow fast, making your space feel more secluded.

All in all, vertical gardens are trendy right now because people have made them so. We're always looking for what's next, what's new, and living walls are it at the moment. You can't scroll through social media without seeing several photos of millennials in front of living walls. So, they are trendy, but your main question might still be, why do I need one (or more) of those?

Read on.

Why Choose a Vertical Garden?

So far, we've covered health benefits, ecological benefits, and aesthetics. There is another advantage to vertical gardens, though, and that is practicality. If the reasons above aren't enough to convince you that this is something you need, then you might want to look at the practical reasons why a vertical garden would improve your life.

Vertical gardens can be more than decorative pieces; you can grow your own vegetables, fruits, herbs, and flowers on them as well. Without much effort, you'll have what you need from the farmer's market right on your doorstep – or maybe, your balcony. Besides being aesthetically pleasing, your vertical garden can also feed you, and again, you don't need a green thumb to make it happen.

When used for growing crops, the greatest thing about vertical gardens is that they're easy to both maintain and harvest. And you can grow a multitude of vegetables and herbs in a very small amount of space. If you have a big backyard, you might opt for a traditional garden, but the vertical garden is the way to go for those who do not have space. If you think your family and friends will love your new beautiful vertical wall, imagine telling them it also gives you the ingredients you need to make tasty family meals.

The question here shouldn't be, "Is this for me?" It should be, "Why hadn't I done this sooner?" Maybe you're being introduced to vertical gardens for the first time, or maybe you simply didn't know where to start. This is the book that will guide you and teach you everything you need to know about creating your very own vertical garden. This is the incentive you need to start now. Keep reading to find out more about vertical gardens and learn the answers to the questions that may have popped into your mind. Next, we're talking about how to choose the right place for your vertical garden.

Chapter 2: Where to Place Your Vertical Garden

In the previous chapter, we learned some things about vertical gardens, such as what they are and the benefits of creating your own. We also discussed the different dwellings that can make use of vertical gardens. In this chapter, we'll take a further look at where you should place your vertical garden. We'll consider areas that will benefit your plants and which plants are the best depending on specific conditions.

We have discussed various areas where a vertical garden or living wall would do very well due to its ecological and health benefits. Still, I promised you more, so here is a more detailed list of a few more areas and why these non-traditional gardens can add something valuable to them. Several case studies have been conducted to determine why and if vertical gardens work in these areas, and the results have been extremely promising. I'll mention some of those famous places below.

Vertical Gardens at Airports

Airports, much like hospitals, are one of those places that are aesthetically bland and lack color. They both serve specific purposes, and making their infrastructure look appealing is not one of their top priorities. Even though we can all understand this, airports worldwide have been stepping up their game by making smart and ecologically sound decisions that also add to their attractiveness and uniqueness. They've been incorporating living walls into their most bland, unimaginative spaces.

From boarding gates to the VIP lounges, some airports worldwide have added living walls to their spaces. Beyond their beauty, they also provide cleaner and safer air quality and help calm the travel-weary passengers. If you're ever in New Zealand or London, you can keep an eye out for them at Christchurch Airport or Heathrow Airport, respectively.

Bringing a piece of the outdoors inside is an incredibly effective method of making passengers want to spend more time at those locations, often choosing to fly predominantly from those airports and even spending larger amounts of time there before catching their flight. This usually translates to more money spent at duty-free shops, restaurants, and cafés. It's simple; if people are comfortable, they'll want to stay longer.

Vertical Gardens in Courtyards

I can't think of anything more relaxing or soothing than to spend an afternoon outdoors surrounded by nature. In busy cities, having a little bit of nature in your apartment complex or shared office courtyards acts as an incentive to enjoy the benefits of being outdoors. Aside from increasing your Vitamin D levels by dint of being outdoors, the calming effects of living walls can boost your mood and productivity.

Spending your lunch break near a living wall can give you what you need to continue your afternoon feeling more upbeat and positive, which helps you be more productive at work. Even a small living wall can improve courtyards, and people who frequent them would benefit from them tremendously.

Vertical Gardens in Rooftop Bars

I've told you all about the amazing benefits of having your own vertical garden right on your balcony, but rooftops are just as incredible at accommodating one or more of them. If the building you live in or where you work has a mostly-unused rooftop, why not turn it into a beautiful rooftop garden that everyone can enjoy? Moreover, as space is not an issue when dealing with vertical gardens, you won't be taking up any floor space, which means you can have a few benches or seats set out for everyone.

This trend has become popular among rooftop bars, where space is limited, and it helps create a sense of privacy from other nearby buildings. Plus, who doesn't enjoy drinking a cocktail in a chic environment that feels like you're in the middle of nature?

Vertical Gardens at Events

As more and more people are using out-of-the-box ideas to make their events unique, many have opted for living walls as their primary focus. Whether you are planning a birthday or an annual company party, a living wall will elevate the event while acting as a fabulous backdrop for photos, which can generate more interest in your event.

Some business events usually call for something different, exciting, and new because they have competitors trying to sell the same product or service. These types of events can gain the most from something as unique as a living wall. You can even customize the wall, choosing plants with colors and textures that suit your business' logo or vision.

Vertical Gardens Used for Branding

Aside from being a great way to make your business events unique, you can also consider using living walls for branding. If an eco-friendly approach is part of your business or products, sell it by making it known that you care about the environment. Creating sublime living walls is the easiest way to show off how forward-thinking your company is. It'll be a great addition to your building, and if you need any inspiration, the H&M headquarters in London has already done this. Brands like Nike, The Body Shop, and Volkswagen have adopted this branding technique as well.

Vertical Gardens in Public Spaces

Some cities have been utilizing living walls to make public spaces feel more welcoming. Places like train stations, car parks, markets, and public buildings like the post office are more enjoyable when they don't look like big cement blocks. Making public spaces more unique makes inhabitants feel happier, which can entice them to live in that city or near those spaces. It's not every day you see a living wall adorning your local train station, so imagine the smile on your face when you do.

Vertical gardens are a must in large cities. Adding them to public spaces will improve the city's aesthetics and inhabitants' health.

Vertical Gardens in Restaurants and Bars

Restaurants and bars nowadays are not only about the food or drinks they serve. In our society, the vibe and feel of a place are a vital part of every customer's experience there. Going out to eat or for a drink has become more about the general experience rather than just about the food and drinks you get. People are chasing what's new and contemporary and want something exciting to look forward to. This is why many restaurants and bars are adding living walls to their designs.

Some places, such as the Facebook Office in Dublin and the Crystal Serenity Cruises offices in the United States of America, have incorporated living walls in their space to give their customers a new dining experience. When used in bars, a living wall can also mean storing and growing your own herbs for cocktails and drinks, adding a fun and practical level to your clients' experience.

Vertical Gardens at Universities and Schools

We've already covered some of the positive effects of living walls, such as the ones they have on our stress levels, productivity, and rational or logical thinking. Incorporating these works of art into universities or secondary schools can increase motivation and decrease depression in students, especially if the living walls are located near libraries or lecture halls.

Students can feel more relaxed throughout their exams and study periods and experience the sensation of being outside, which will be beneficial, especially when they have to spend hours on end studying indoors.

Choosing the optimal wall or location in your space is important when creating these living walls. It requires some thinking and planning to find the optimal location, but fear not! The place you've been thinking about might just be the perfect one if you have the right tools, plants, and knowledge. One of the most important things to consider is how to keep your plants alive, so let's discuss that.

Keeping Your Living Walls Alive

When thinking of plants, water is likely to be one of the first things to cross your mind, and rightly so; watering your living wall, just like your potted plants, is necessary. There are a few different ways you can go about this, and you should consider them carefully before deciding where you want your living wall to be and what types of plants or herbs you want to grow.

Depending on your chosen system, you will have more or less flexibility as to which plants you can grow. As technology advances, you can also find various systems to use, some of which are more affordable than others. The less work you will have to do daily equals a higher price tag on your watering system. You can take the simplest route and water your vertical garden yourself, manually, but this method can take up a lot of time and effort, so be prepared.

The next section of the book describes the most common systems. Each one has its advantages and disadvantages; it's up to you to consider which type of vertical garden you want and the amount of time you can dedicate to it, while also keeping in mind the cost and efficiency levels.

Drip Irrigation System

This system is most efficient for your living wall because it uses a hydroponic system connected to your plumbing. This can be a problem, though, if you don't have a water source near your balcony or driveway. On a positive note, one major advantage of drip irrigation systems is that they can recycle water, which makes them more sustainable than other systems. You can reuse water from an air-conditioning unit, a coffee machine, or even the water you use to wash your vegetables.

Drip irrigation systems entail higher start-up costs but require less labor, which makes them quite efficient.

Tank System

Tank systems use replaceable trays; the soiled water in the trays has to be changed often. Unfortunately, they are not allowed in hospitals or places with strict hygiene codes to follow because they require more water and soil. This soil may lead to the appearance of pests and diseases that are not compatible with these types of facilities. This is a drawback not found in the drip irrigation systems mentioned earlier.

Tank systems also require more maintenance, such as frequent soil changes to prevent fungus and mold. This can be a deal-breaker for busy beginners.

Whichever system you go for, you'll also need to know which types of plants you'd be able to grow as each one is different and will, therefore, need specific care and maintenance.

What Type of Plants Should You Choose?

The list is extensive and varied. Are you thinking about aesthetics, practicality, or the difficulty of maintenance? Depending on your available time, budget, and needs, you'll be faced with many choices that should be taken into consideration when creating your vertical garden.

Whether you go for plants, herbs, vegetables, or fruit, you need to keep in mind the exact location they'll be living in and if they'll be happy growing near each other. Let's say you choose plants that grow at very different rates; you'll find that your little ones might not even grow at all, as they'll be overshadowed by the bigger ones and not have as much access to light as they need. If you choose woodier plants, which are thicker and heavier, you won't get that beautiful garden flow since they do not fall delicately downwards. With lighter plants like flowers or vines, you'll get that cascading effect that looks bushier and more appealing to the eye.

Another point to consider when choosing the right plants is whether you want to grow any fruits or vegetables. Not every fruit or vegetable can be grown successfully in a vertical garden. Some smaller-sized fruits and vegetables will thrive in these conditions. Larger produce such as apples or pumpkins is just not cut out for vertical gardening.

You have a lot of thinking to do before starting your own vertical garden. In Chapter Six, you'll find a more detailed explanation of which plants to choose based on the different specifications and a glossary to help you make your choice.

Choosing the right plants is important. What's just as important is giving them the right amount of sunlight. Let's take a quick look at that.

Sunlight vs. Shade

As you already know, vertical gardens can easily grow indoors; they need not be outside to survive. Sunlight is always important, so even if your vertical garden will be inside your home, you must consider what type of natural light it'll be exposed to.

One of the best tips is to never choose a spot fully exposed to sunlight or fully shaded from it. This will give you more flexibility when deciding on which plants to grow. This is the next most important factor to consider aside from your watering system, which we've already discussed. Even if you have plants that don't require a lot of exposure to sunlight, they may still need to be watered often, so finding a balance that suits your lifestyle will lead to a more successful vertical garden.

If your preferred location is not always exposed to sunlight, consider buying modular containers so that you can move them around as needed. This is especially useful if a plant is not doing so well in its location, and you wish to move that specific one instead of the entire vertical garden.

Most plants will include information on their bag or tag regarding the exposure and water levels they need, so make sure you look at that and keep this information in mind when starting your vertical garden.

In the next chapter, we'll look at how to pick the right soil for your plants.

Chapter 3: Picking the Right Soil

We've talked about some basics of vertical gardening, and in this chapter, we're looking at another important part of all types of gardening: picking the right soil. When starting your vertical garden or living wall, you have to start right at the base, the soil, before getting to the pretty plants, bright flowers, and luscious greens.

When it comes to choosing your soil, there are two different approaches. The most common one is to know what plants, flowers, fruits, or vegetables you want to grow and then choose the right soil for them. The other approach is to first pick your soil depending on your budget and then find plants that are compatible with that soil type. The second method is less common, but it may be suitable for some people.

Let's find out what types of soil exist and what soils some plants prefer so that you can keep that in mind when choosing your own.

Soil Types

The different soil types for your vertical garden or living wall are the same ones used for any type of gardening in general; it's all just soil. But the plants you choose will determine the best soil type for your vertical garden.

The different basic types of soil are:
1. Sandy soil
2. Clay
3. Silt
4. Peat
5. Chalky soil
6. Loam

Sandy Soil:

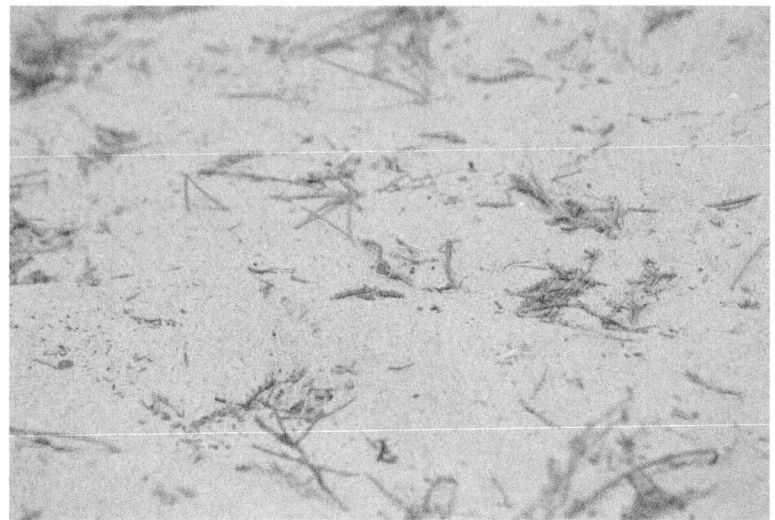

Ryan Mascarenhas, CC BY-SA 4.0 <https://creativecommons.org/licenses/by-sa/4.0>, via Wikimedia Commons https://commons.wikimedia.org/wiki/File:Sandy_soil.jpg

This type of soil is considered "light" soil; it has a high amount of sand and a low amount of clay, and sand is lighter than clay. It is also warm and dry and doesn't have many nutrients. Sandy soil can be easy to work with for a beginner, but it dries out in the summer, and the low amount of nutrients that it does have are easily washed away by water. It can be useful, though, if you're looking for a type of soil with quick water drainage.

Sandy soil can be improved with organic matter, which gives plants the nutrients they need. Growing herbs in this type of soil works well, so if you'd like to have your own herb garden with rosemary, salvia, or lavender, sandy soil might be the right soil for your vertical garden.

Clay:

https://pixabay.com/es/photos/tierra-suelo-arcilloso-arcilla-298042/

Clay soil is on the opposite end of the spectrum from sandy soil. It contains high amounts of nutrients and is lumpy and sticky when wet but hard and smooth when dry, which makes it difficult to cultivate, especially if you're a beginner. Also, in contrast with sandy soil, clay soil is a slow-draining soil, so it keeps its nutrients, making it a good choice for plant growth.

This type of soil will definitely test your new skills and might not be the best choice for a vertical garden due to its weight; however, if you use it in a horizontal garden, sunflowers, cabbages, and broccoli thrive in clay soils.

Silt:

https://pixabay.com/es/photos/tierra-suelo-seco-textura-3622038/

Silt is smooth to the touch and has a soapy consistency when it's moist. It is considered light soil but retains moisture better than sandy soil, so it has a higher amount of nutrients and is more fertile. Because its soil particles are medium-sized and fine, the soil structure is easily compacted. While it does retain its moisture, this means it retains the cold and drains poorly. It is nonetheless an easier soil to grow plants in than clay soil.

While not ideal for vertical gardening, lettuce and artichokes like silt, as do cabbages and even rice. The first two can be grown in a vertical garden; growing either or both of the second two entails special considerations.

Peat:

Ragesoss, CC BY-SA 3.0 <https://creativecommons.org/licenses/by-sa/3.0>, via Wikimedia Commons https://commons.wikimedia.org/wiki/File:Schultz_Sphagnum_Peat_Moss.jpg

Peat soil is dark and soft to the touch. It has a high amount of organic matter but is low in nutrients. It retains water very well and may need extra care with drainage. The advantage of this is that it'll keep its moisture during the dry months, and even though this is not the type of soil you easily find in your garden, it is a great choice for planting.

Flowers love this soil, and ferns, camellias, and azaleas are the perfect match for peat soils.

Chalky Soil:

Chalky soils may not be the best for plant growth as they're alkaline (meaning they have a higher pH level), preventing many plants from growing in them. Ericaceous plants such as azaleas, camellias, hydrangeas, or some types of berries, hate chalky soil.

Because this soil is also free-draining, any minerals in it will be drawn away quickly by water, which means most plants will have a hard time growing. You can add fertilizers to this soil to make it more manageable for beginners. Some plants that do well in chalky soils are ivy, grapevines, and clematis.

Loam:

Loam is considered the best type of soil for growing plants. It's a mixture of silt, clay, and sand; it retains moisture well, but it also drains well – it's truly the perfect mix of soil. It has many nutrients due to the balance of the three types of soil, and it warms up easily in spring but doesn't dry out in summer like other types. For an easier time growing your vertical garden or living wall, loamy soil is the best to start with. You should always add organic matter or extra nutrients to it, but it is the easiest to manage.

As it's a gardener's best friend, loam can be used with most plants and flowers that don't require any of the specific characteristics of the other types of soil.

I've mentioned that different nutrients are needed by different plants, and you've probably been wondering what nutrients or organic matter are the most suitable for your plants. Let's have a look at that.

What Nutrients do Plants Need?

Simply put, plants need potassium, nitrogen, and phosphorus for growth. There are other important nutrients, such as calcium, sulfur, magnesium, and even metallic elements such as iron, manganese, zinc, and copper, but the first three are the main nutrients your plants are going to need to grow well.

Each nutrient has a different purpose, but the main three (called "NPK," after their designations on the periodic table) will give your plant healthier leaves and increase its longevity. If your plant's leaves are darker than normal and there's a loss of leaves, you might be looking at a phosphorus deficiency. If the upper leaves are light green and the lower ones are yellow and shriveled, then your plant probably lacks nitrogen. And if you see yellowing at the tips of your plant's leaves, it wants potassium.

As you can see, each nutrient contributes to a different aspect of a plant's health and appearance; making sure your soil has the right balance of nutrients will result in healthier, better-looking plants.

Adding Nutrients to Your Soil (Organically)

Now that you're aware of how important nutrients are for plant growth, let's talk about what you can do to add them to your soil organically. There are many ways to do this that won't break the bank.

- **Leaf Litter** - You can collect leaves around your garden or city area and use them to make compost or use them directly on your soil as mulch. When used this way, leaf litter will block weeds and increase moisture while slowly adding nutrients to your plant's soil.

- **Grass Clippings** - These are a great addition as they provide a lot of nitrogen to help keep leaves green and healthy. If you don't have a lawn of your own, you may be able to find collection points in your area where you can get them.

- **Compost** - It doesn't have to be difficult to make compost, and if you use it, your soil will use it all up. Use a mixture of grass clippings or weeds as your base, as they are high in nitrogen, with leaf litter or straw, as they are high in carbon. Those two nutrients combined will make the perfect addition to your soil.

- **Straw** - Even though this is a potentially expensive method of adding nutrients to your soil, it can be a good choice for those who have it.

- **Wood Chips** - This is a similar option to leaf litter in that it can be used as mulch. Wood chips decompose more slowly, so keep that in mind. They can also be added to your compost bin, as they are high in carbon.

- **Cover Crops** - Crops like vetch or clover are easily accessible, and they add nitrogen to the soil as they grow. Cover crops also work well because they attract pollinators.

- **Wood Ashes** - These add potassium to the soil, which prevents the yellowing of leaves. Wood ashes are especially great if you own a wood stove, as you'll already have them. Be careful if using them, as they can be a limiting agent. They're also less effective than commercially-bought lime if you're trying to raise the soil's pH levels.
- **Manure** - Manure is high in phosphorus, which will help with your plants' growth and health.

Starting by experimenting with any of these will teach you what's best for the soil you buy or use. It's not an exact science, as most soils vary from one area to another and from brand to brand, so don't worry too much; experimenting is part of owning a vertical garden or living wall, and if you ask me, it's the best part.

After deciding on the right type of soil and nutrients to add to it, you may be thinking, "But how much will I need?" This is a great question.

How Much Soil Do You Need?

You might just want to wing it and buy a few bags of potting soil and figure it out once you've started planting, but I wouldn't recommend that. You might end up with too much, or you might not have enough. Nobody wants to run to the garden center a second time to get more soil, especially when they're excited to start this journey into the world of vertical gardening and living walls. Thankfully, it's easy to find out how much soil you need before you start.

Whether you have a large or small container for your plants, the formula for soil volume in a rectangular or square-shaped container is easy to calculate. Start by measuring its length, width, and height in feet (or fractions of feet). The volume of the container is the product of multiplying those three measurements, which gives you a result in cubic feet. Once you get that number, divide it by 27 to get the exact number of cubic yards you need to buy.

Volume = Length x Width x Height (in feet)

Volume/27 = amount of soil to buy (in cubic yards)

If your container is not a rectangle or square, you may treat it as such to get the most approximate measurements. Err on the side of caution and round up, so that you have enough soil instead of having to go back to the store.

Preparation is key when taking up gardening; the more you know, the better you'll be able to handle problems when they arise. The same goes for preparing your vertical garden or living wall. There are different things to consider and prepare before you start planting. Let's look at a few of those things next.

Things to Consider When Preparing for a Vertical Garden

Besides everything else already mentioned, it's important to decide which structure you want to use to grow your vertical garden or living wall. You can buy containers or a freestanding structure, or even make your own.

If you decide to make your own vertical garden supporting structure, consider the materials from which you can build your structure. These structures can be made of wood, metal, plastic, iron, or a mixture of these materials. A very common structure utilizes an iron frame with wooden planks; this design is sturdy and is easily attached to a wall. If your vertical garden or living wall will be outdoors, consider weatherproofing treatments for both the wood and the metal.

You don't have to build this yourself; nowadays, it's easy to find ready-built or modular structures that suit the space and design concept you're going for. You can even go for a mix of both by buying a few parts and then DIY-ing the rest to adapt it to what you want.

Another factor to consider when preparing to build a vertical garden is to think about the wall or space where you want to place it. Preparing the wall to protect it against the roots of your plants is important, as well as preventing the humidity from the plants from getting into your wall. You'll have to water your plants, and you need to plan it so that you won't be watering your wall every day or every few days. If you're attaching your vertical structure to a wall, use a durable plastic sheet as a moisture barrier between the wall and the supporting structure.

Remember that different irrigation systems and options are available to you; when creating a living wall, having the right irrigation system is incredibly helpful and necessary to the well-being of your plants as well as the wall itself.

For example, if you really want an irrigation system, a drip system will be safer for the drywall and interior-grade paint behind your plants than a waterfall or heavy misting or sprinklers.

It's all about balance, and you can do it if you think of everything ahead of time. To help you make the best decisions, in the next chapter, we'll be talking about the pros and cons of containers, planters, and trellises.

Chapter 4: Containers, Planters, and Trellises

You're almost ready! You have thought about the ideal space for your vertical garden and its level of exposure to sunlight, as well as the right soil for the plants you want to grow. This chapter will help you to decide if you want to use containers, planters, or trellises in your vertical structure.

We'll be looking at the differences between the three options available to you, as well as some exciting, cheap DIYs you can use to add that extra touch your space is lacking.

There are three main options, with subdivisions to consider, so let's find the right one for you.

https://www.pexels.com/photo/six-potted-plants-close-up-photo-1660533/

Containers

Containers can be made of the most imaginative materials as well as the more common ones. Pots are the most commonly used container by gardeners; they're versatile, cheap if made from plastic, and are what most people use in their homes. You can buy them at garden centers and supermarkets, and you can find a wide variety of sizes that suit your needs. I especially love clay pots; I find them pleasing to the eye, and they are a good option for a vertical herb garden. They can be a little heavy, so the structure you use to hang them must be solid.

You can have fun with containers by thinking outside of the box. Even if pots can be relatively cheap, you may want to be more environmentally friendly and recycle some everyday products like plastic bottles or tin cans. By reusing these items, you won't be adding any extra costs to your vertical garden, and they work as well, or better than store-bought standard fare. They are usually lighter than clay or ceramic vases, so this is a good option if you're not very confident about the strength or durability of your vertical structure.

You can even reuse glass jars, which would look beautiful with different shapes, sizes, and colors hanging on a wall. Just remember openings for drainage; glass weep-holes would have to be drilled, not cut or punched out. A trend that has appeared recently is glass terrariums filled with succulents that look great while maintaining moisture levels in the terrarium.

An easy way to create your own containers which are still chic is to use landscape fabric to create little pockets. You then fill these pockets with your soil and seeds, and then you can simply hang them on any wall. I love how simple, easy, cheap, yet strikingly elegant this looks in or outside a home.

Planters

Planters are typically made of wood, and they can have standard garden beds or raised garden beds. Vertical planters can also include the use of rope, hooks, pipes, and wire.

Your creativity can take charge here as you'll decide how to create your vertical planter. You can go for a geometrical feel or a cleaner, industrial vibe. You can also mix and match plants and flowers or add different herbs. You can hang planters from the ceiling, but they can also be attached to a wall using plywood or pipes. Rope is also a commonly used material, and if you are bothered by the appearance of traditional rope, you can find different colors and match them to your plants or containers.

The sky is truly the limit when it comes to your preferences and style. Planters are great because they're effortlessly stunning, whereas, with a tin, plastic, or clay container, you might need to do a little more to it if you're going for a specific look. Moreover, because you have so much freedom over your planter's style, you can easily adapt the materials you use to fit them into your budget. You can even use things you have lying around your home, transforming them into chic

or beautiful planters that will hold your favorite plants.

Trellises

https://pixabay.com/es/photos/reja-de-madera-el-cenador-liana-2501643/

A trellis is a latticework structure usually made from wood, metal, or even bamboo. It is mainly used for plants but can have other uses too. Plants wrap and anchor themselves onto the trellis – sometimes with a little help from us gardeners, which we do by tying them to its framework when they're growing. These architectural structures are beautiful in and of themselves, so even when your plants are just seeds or little sprouts, your vertical garden or living wall will already be looking fantastic.

Another benefit of trellises is that they are very easy to install. They can be used just as a structure of their own to complement garden beds. A trellis can be attached to a wall, too, for a simple way to allow your plants to grow vertically. This is a great option for a living wall to create a privacy screen, as discussed earlier. This will provide you with more intimacy, even when your plants are not fully grown, as the trellis pattern will help conceal your space slightly.

Because a trellis makes your plants interwoven and close together when they've grown, it creates a barrier for noise and wind, and the trellis itself is usually easy to clean. The problems arise when bad weather damages the trellis. Even when they are made of metal, being placed outdoors makes them susceptible to corrosion or rust. This means you'll either have to buy a new one from time to time or apply specific treatments to protect the one you own.

Moreover, if they're exposed to extreme weather conditions, they have the tendency to shrink or bend. A wooden trellis may also grow mold and mildew if not treated properly. These disadvantages may lead to higher costs in maintaining the structure itself, but a trellis is still easy to set up and looks great from day one.

The table below gives you a summary of the pros and cons mentioned for each type of structure. It will hopefully allow for easier comparison between them and help you choose which one to use.

	Containers	Planters	Trellis
Pros	+ Easily moved for better light or shade + Virtually no weed problems + Less risk of soil-borne disease	+ Aesthetically pleasing + Mix and match different plants and succulents + Simple upkeep	+ Stunning from day one + Easy to clean + Perfect for creating privacy in an open or high visibility area

Cons	- A lot of different containers to water if you don't use an irrigation system - Less attractive when just starting out - More preparation required	- Require some creativity - More preparation required - Harder to move as a single unit	- Potential higher cost to maintain - Exposure to the elements leads to structural damages - Mold and mildew may occur

DIYs: Making your Own Containers, Planters, and Trellises

Wire Wall Planter

All you'll need for this DIY project is wire or steel mesh, pots, rings, and hooks. It's that simple!

Wire or steel mesh is a material you can get at most any garden or hardware store. There is a wide variety of sizes, colors, and patterns. This part is fun as you can choose a common trellis shape, a crisscross or lozenge shape, or go for something totally different like simple squares. It's up to you!

The pots you choose can be made of clay, plastic, or ceramic. Because you'll be attaching the wire mesh to a wall, the structure will be solid enough for heavier pots. Make sure your pots have a hole at the bottom for draining water. Keep in mind that because they'll be hanging, you won't be able to add a pot tray underneath them.

The hooks will connect your pots to the wire mesh.

Follow the instructions below to make this quick and easy DIY wire wall planter:

1. Place the wire mesh against the wall and drill a few holes just below the top edge of the wireframe. The heavier the pots, the more holes and hooks you'll need to ensure it's durable.
2. Add wall plugs to the drilled holes for a more stable structure.
3. Once done, screw hooks into the wall plugs. The hooks will support the wire mesh.
4. After that, hang your wire mesh. Make sure it's level and tightened to your liking.
5. Hang the pots using hooks and rings to go around each pot.
6. Voilà! Your vertical wall is ready!

To make your planter more unique and eye-catching, paint the wall behind it or even add some colorful rope along the wire – but be sure to do this before your plants are fully grown. You can also add a garden bed below the planter (if it's outdoors) and grow climbing plants that will use the wire mesh as their support – a simple and beautiful idea to DIY your first vertical garden.

Recycled Bottles

Going with a simpler and cheaper method, recycled bottles are easy to use and very accessible. You won't need many materials, and this DIY project can be done in just under an hour or so, depending on how large you want this project to be.

The materials you'll need for this are very straightforward:

- Plastic bottles, empty and clean
- Scissors

Thread, wire, or rope Follow the instructions below to make this easy, environmentally friendly DIY planter:

1. After cleaning your plastic bottles thoroughly, cut a large, rectangular hole on one side of your bottle. This is where your seedlings will go and where your plants will grow out of.

2. Then, make two tiny holes on each side of the rectangle you just cut out. These four tiny holes will be used to pass your thread, wire, or rope to ensure your container is well secured.
3. Once you've passed the cordage through the two left and two right holes, tie a large knot to hold the bottle in place. Decide what spacing you want between each bottle, then repeat.
4. Last, make two or three weep-holes at the bottom of the container to permit drainage.
5. Hang it all on a wall using strong hooks, or nail it, and you're done!

This incredibly simple DIY project means that you can start this today, right now. We all have a few extra bottles lying around the house, and this is the project to use them in!

Shoe Organizer Vertical Garden

As strange as this DIY project may sound, it actually works very well and is a simple way to create a vegetable or herb garden in your kitchen or on your balcony. This is a list of what you'll need for this project:

- A hanging shoe organizer (which has several pockets)
- A pole or pipe with its respective attachments
- Strong hanging hooks
- Wood plank (optional)
- A tray or garden bed (optional)

You can hang this shoe organizer garden wherever you want. Depending on the weight it must support and the wall material to which you'll be screwing it, use the right tools and anchors so that your vertical structure is sturdy. Follow the instructions below to do this creative DIY project:

1. Attach the pole or pipe (a curtain pole, for example) to the wall.

2. Use the strong hooks to hold the shoe organizer and connect it to the pole or pipe you've mounted. Remember that even if the storage pouch may be light, with the added soil, plants, and water, it will get heavy. The hooks need to support all that total weight.
3. Then, to check drainage, pour water into each pocket. If there's no visible drainage, make a few holes in them.
4. Once it's all done, add your soil and plants, and it's ready.
5. An optional step is to push the vertical garden away from a wall by drilling or gluing a wood plank onto the wall behind the structure. For a more environmentally friendly option, use a pot tray or even a garden bed below your structure so that the excess water from the pockets drains into it. This means that less water will be wasted as it will water the plants below.

Who would have known that such a simple product like a shoe organizer could have such a fun purpose as well?

Pallet Planter

This DIY is the easiest and cheapest one yet. All you need is a pallet (or two, or more depending on the size of your vertical garden) and a few containers of your choice. You won't have to change the pallet at all, but you should paint or weatherproof it if attaching it to a wall or solid structure outside.

You'll use the bottom side of the pallet as it has spaces between the wood slats, and these will act as shelves. If you can get them, euro pallets are the best for this DIY project as they come with three shelves, and each shelf has two rectangular openings that will accommodate one container. If you have difficulty finding the right sized container for the openings, tack a wood slat over the shelf opening to reduce its size to something closer to that of the container.

This DIY project will be a great start for your vertical garden. It can help you test the waters and get the hang of things before moving onto something bigger and more costly.

Whether you buy or make your vertical garden or living wall structure, you'll have the means to grow your own plants, vegetables, fruit, or flowers. With the knowledge in this chapter, you'll be better prepared to make an informed decision when it comes to how much or how little effort you want to put into your vertical garden project before you get started. One thing I'm sure of is that you should have some fun while doing it and also that you're more than capable of doing one or all of these **DIY** projects!

Starting your vertical garden or living wall need not be a daunting task. You can do it right now. Using the information in this book, and a little effort and passion, in just a few weeks, you can be drinking your morning coffee or tea, looking at your new green wall, and wondering how you could have ever lived without it for so long.

In the next chapter, we'll revisit a few points and summarize a list of things you need to start your vertical garden.

Chapter 5: The Vertical Gardening Start-Up

By now, you're probably feeling excited and confident about starting your new hobby, gardening. You're feeling even more thrilled about covering up that ugly, blank wall you've had in your home for far too long. You're ready to get your hands dirty - literally, as they'll be covered in soil - and you can't wait to get started. So, to make sure you're ready, we will go through all the different steps and things you need to get everything up and running.

This will be a recap and summary of everything you need to think about and decide on in order to have a successful start. Use this chapter as a guide through the different options and ideas available to you. It will help you find the best options for your situation and serve as a reminder that you're in charge, and your creativity will lead you wherever you allow it to.

Use this as a checklist (as well as the real checklist at the end of the chapter) to get started. Tick off things as you go, and you'll be a step closer to getting this done right. Let's go through these options and steps together.

Installing Your First Vertical Garden

Choose Your Wall/Spot

This should go without saying, but here I am, saying it. Before any plans are made, or any DIY projects are started, you need to know exactly where you want your vertical garden to go. Consider the spot for its purpose. Is it a sunny wall that happens to get too hot early in the afternoon, and you need a way to cool it down? Is it a way to get some privacy from neighbors directly across from you? Or is it a sustainable way to grow some of your own produce?

The purpose of this garden will dictate which wall or spot you choose, so think about it carefully. Once you have decided on it, consider the different ways you can hang or place a vertical garden in that space. Will it be okay for you to drill into it? Is it a strong enough wall to have heavy containers hanging off of it? If you're renting, do you have permission to do so? If your spot is indoors, think about potential humidity issues since you don't want to damage any furniture or walls with your newfound passion.

Once your spot is chosen and you're sure you can make it happen there, you'll be able to choose your type of containers, trellis, and even plants because you'll know what the conditions of that spot are.

What Plants Are You Going to Choose?

The next step is a fun one! Plants, vegetables, herbs, flowers, or fruit? You now get to choose what you want to grow and see in your vertical garden. You can choose by color or size, and if going for herbs, you can even grow new ones to test them in your favorite dishes.

Since you already know the location of your vertical garden, you'll get to make an informed decision on what plants or produce are the best to plant. This is the easiest way to create your first vertical garden as you don't find yourself needing to move it around later on. Sometimes, moving it around isn't even an option as your garden might be too heavy, or you just don't have space anywhere else. Choosing what plants you can grow in the chosen spot is the way to ensure a successful start.

To learn more about plants and which ones are the best choice for you, read Chapter 6, where you'll find a detailed list of the best plants for your vertical garden and living wall. This includes information about soil, watering, and how to plant them.

The Right Soil for Your Plants

Knowing which plants you want to grow will make the choice of soil easy. This is because each plant requires a specific type of soil with more or fewer nutrients, more or fewer fertilizers, and even more or less water.

This decision should be made after picking which plants or flowers you prefer. This will give you a wider variety of colors and plant types to choose from for the vertical garden of your dreams. However, if you don't want to bother with different soil types because of specific plant requirements, you can choose plants that all need the same type of soil. This may limit your options in plant selection, but it may also help you as a beginner not to get mixed up.

Whichever path you'll take, this is a decision you cannot skip as the soil is the base, the home for your plants, and it will directly impact how well they will grow and flourish.

To Fertilize or Not to Fertilize

If you have some doubts on whether to use fertilizers or not, you may check Chapter 3, where we discussed it thoroughly. Helping your soil by adding necessary nutrients to it may determine the successful growth of your plants. Even if the soil you choose is the right one for a plant, it doesn't mean it has everything it needs to flourish. Nutrients will give it that extra boost, especially when it's still a sprout.

When drainage is not an issue, your type of soil might allow water to wash away many of its nutrients; therefore, your plant will not thrive. You may not be at fault – soils all have a different percentage of nutrients; even identical bags of store-bought potting soil are all slightly different in this regard. So, adding some nutrients will help prevent that nutrient loss or just give your plants a boost they'll be happy to get.

You can go fully organic and environmentally friendly by reusing materials available to you, or you can get them store-bought. Choosing to fertilize shouldn't be a question, and the options for fertilizer are endless – just re-read Chapter 3 for some ideas on how to fertilize your plants.

Where to Grow: Containers or Trellis

The next step on your checklist should be to decide whether you prefer containers, planters, or a trellis. Any of these is an amazing option. There isn't one better than the others in general, but there should be a clear winner to you, depending on the space you have and where you'll place your vertical garden.

If your vertical garden is on your very small balcony, I'd say a trellis is probably the way to go. It will take up a tiny bit of floor space. If you use containers, there is a chance they will take up a bit more volume. One way around this is to hang them, in which case you can keep your floor space free for other things.

You may also be thinking about the aesthetics. Do you want a freestanding trellis to decorate a patio? Do you prefer a modern approach, using concrete containers that contrast with the green of the plants? Maybe you're even considering both: a couple of raised garden beds underneath a trellis attached to a wall.

Now that you know your chosen spot well and the type of plants you want to grow, making this decision should be easier. Just remember that it's your space, and you're the one who needs to love it. Whether convenience, beauty, or practicality, you're in charge.

Don't Forget the Gardening Tools

We haven't talked about them yet, so you'll be pleased to know that you don't have to buy a huge supply of gardening tools, nor do you need to buy any top-of-the-line ones. Start with the basics, and as you go along, you'll get more or better tools that will help make your job easier.

For a first-time vertical gardener, I would get the following gardening tools: gardening gloves, gardening fork, garden trowel, shears, pruners, scissors, and a watering can (a hose will work fine if you're outside). If you feel like spending time working in your garden is something you will often do and don't have old clothes, invest in an apron.

These tools will help you maneuver the soil, move things around, and water your plants (if you choose not to have an automatic irrigation system). They will also help you take care of your vertical garden in the long run, as you'll need to prune certain plants from time to time. You need not get the most expensive tools to start; a cheap, plastic version will do just fine at first.

Should You Decorate Your Vertical Garden?

This is an added step that is entirely optional. It's if you want to go the extra mile and jazz up your vertical garden or living wall a little more. You can do different things to make it even more interesting to look at. Sometimes just the way you place your containers will create a stunning, eye-catching piece of décor.

You can do a little or a lot with your space, and decorating it might just help give it that extra touch of beauty. For example, if you decide to use the recycled bottles project discussed in chapter four, you may want to paint them a unique color. Pink or black will contrast well with the green of the plants. If you have colorful flowers planted in your living wall, then you can also tie them together with a background color.

You could also add lights above your vertical garden or living wall to make it stand out even more. Colored LEDs are also very trendy right now and can be easily placed around your living wall. You could also hang a long container high up on your wall and let the plants or flowers flow downwards at different levels to create a magical look. You could even go as far as using ornate frames around your containers to make them stand out even more.

Your decorations don't have to be too complicated, though. Something as simple as adding small stones or pebbles at the bottom of clear containers will create a modern and chic look, with the added benefit of helping your soil's drainage. You can also think outside of the box, literally, and extend the style you currently have inside your home into your vertical garden. It'll be worth it.

Watering Your Plants: Manually, Automatic Irrigation, or a Mix of Both?

You'll have to consider this step carefully before going ahead with the project because it can impact your budget. Moreover, it may also alter what type of structure you want to get if you choose an irrigation system that is better applied to a specific type of vertical structure. Don't worry though, since you're planning ahead, you still have some flexibility. You'll have the opportunity to adapt and change your mind before you set out on this task.

When considering how to water your plants, you should think about how much time you'd like to spend taking care of your plants. There will always be routine maintenance, but watering plants can be done easily without the need for a watering can.

Utilizing an irrigation system gives you the freedom to spend less time taking care of your plants. There are a few different irrigation systems, from simple to more complex models, cheaper to more expensive, etc.

There's a gravity-fed drip irrigation system. This involves a traditional drip irrigation system using a tank or water container at the top of your garden, which simply lets gravity do its work. If you have a tiered layer system, the drip method only needs to drip water onto the top containers. The water from those will subsequently drip onto the next ones until the extra water falls into a draining tray.

If you want a more complex system because your plants need regular watering, you might consider adding watering pipes on every row of your vertical garden. This involves a higher functioning system where you'll be sure that every plant gets the amount of water it needs. You can even install a timer to control when and for how long water is released, making the system more precise when watering your vertical garden.

You can also use a mixture of both types of systems where you manually deliver water to the top row of your plants while they'll drain the water onto the next row and so on. This involves more time and work on your part, but it's easier than having to water every single one of your containers, especially when you have a very large vertical garden.

Let's look at a simple DIY drip irrigation system that you can install in your vertical garden.

Juandev, CC BY-SA 3.0 <https://creativecommons.org/licenses/by-sa/3.0>, via Wikimedia Commons https://commons.wikimedia.org/wiki/File:Rishpon,_Shefa_Farm,_drip_irrigation_at_work.JPG

DIYing a Drip Irrigation System

To make your very own gravity drip irrigation system, make sure you have the following supplies:

- A water tank
- Malleable pipes, such as a hose or water distribution pipes, with only one end open
- Water emitters
- A timer

The water tank should be installed above your vertical garden, as this drip irrigation system uses gravity to function. The pipes, which must be malleable enough to bend from row to row, will be connected to the opening of the water tank and placed on the soil of each container. Once you've found the right place and secured the pipe as needed, you'll attach the water emitters to where you want your plants to be watered. You can add as many as you want, and these usually have a pressure fit system to make it easier for you to insert them. You can also adjust the amount of water that is delivered through the water emitters. This is done by using a timer to water your plants a specific amount at regular intervals instead of having them running continuously.

As promised, here is your start-up vertical gardening checklist:

- Wall or spot
- Your favorite plants
- Right soil for your plants
- The most suitable fertilizer for you
- Containers or Trellis
- Gardening tools
- Decoration (optional)

- Watering method

If you've ticked all of the boxes above, congratulations! You're ready to start your journey into vertical gardening and living walls. In the next few chapters, we'll dive into the best plants, fruits, veggies, and flowers for your vertical structure. They will give you all the information you need to choose the best ones for you and your space. Be sure to read those before you go off to buy your first plants.

Chapter 6: Best Plants for Your Vertical Garden

Getting the best plants for your vertical garden requires a few steps. You should choose the ones you love, and if we're talking about herbs, the ones you currently use in your dishes. An herb may be fun to plant, but it'll just take up space if you don't use it. That said, because we're dealing with a vertical garden, it's better to choose plants on the smaller side with minimal root systems. These plants won't need as much soil, so everything is lighter when hung up on your structure.

Another question you have to consider is what type of herbs or plants grow well together. Will you grow them in the same container, or should you separate some of them for optimal growth? Sunlight and water are also things you need to think about. If an herb needs more light, it should be placed on the top row. However, if that herb needs more water, it should go at the bottom to collect the most water if you're using a layered row system.

You'll also need to remember to replace certain herbs every year (or more often in some cases) if they seem overgrown. If they are overgrown, the roots will fill up their container, which stresses those plants. Therefore, it's better to keep them on rotation by having extra containers and swapping them as needed. This way, you'll have a beautiful vertical garden all year round.

But let's take a look at what herbs you should include in your vertical garden and which ones may be the best for you.

In the glossary below, you'll find the best herbs for your vertical garden:

1. Basil
2. Chives
3. Cilantro
4. Dill
5. Lavender
6. Marjoram
7. Mint
8. Oregano
9. Parsley
10. Rosemary
11. Sage
12. Tarragon
13. Thyme

Basil

https://www.pexels.com/photo/a-bowl-of-spinach-159094/

Who doesn't love pesto? And if you don't, there are many other ways to use basil in your cooking. This herb is an incredibly fragrant one that loves full sun and grows well alongside tomatoes. In just a few weeks, you'll be able to harvest your first leaves, which is something you should do regularly to keep it going strong.

To plant basil, you can start with the seedlings inside your home, where it's warmer. You can do this for up to six weeks before the temperature rises. Basil likes its soil to be warmer than 50°F, so plan well, and don't forget that temperatures tend to drop at night. Basil should get 6 to 8 hours of full sun daily to grow well. To make sure it gets enough sunlight, this can be one of the plants you keep on your top rows.

- Plant the seeds about a quarter of an inch into the soil, spaced 10 to 12 inches apart.
- The soil should be moist, as basil loves moisture. This is why a vertical garden is great for this plant because it allows greater drainage. Basil prefers moist but well-drained soil.
- Once you see a few leaves, prune to above the second set to encourage more branches to grow. Repeat this every time, pruning it back to its first set of leaves.

Chives

https://pxhere.com/en/photo/838539

Chives bloom in the summer with the most amazing colors, and they're a great addition to dips or sauces. However, be careful when planting them as they are an invasive type of plant and will take over other ones. If you're using a shoe organizer or pocket system, you won't have this issue. They love cooler temperatures, so you can plant them in the fall or spring as long as the temperature of the soil is around 65° F. They take their time to germinate, so don't be worried if you don't get results in the first couple of weeks. They need full sun, but they may also do okay in light shade. Their soil needs to be moist, well-draining, and very rich in nutrients, so incorporate fertilizers freely.

- Plant the seeds about a quarter of an inch into the soil, spaced 2 inches apart.
- Keep the soil thoroughly moist, and if you can see their bulbs (they grow near the surface), cover them with mulch to keep them moist too.
- The flower's seeds spread easily, so if you want to limit your planting area, remove their flowers once they bloom.

Cilantro or Coriander

https://pixabay.com/es/photos/ensalada-cilantro-cocinando-comer-2850199/

You may have heard of this plant being referred to as cilantro, or maybe you heard people calling it coriander... the fact is they're the same! Cilantro refers to the plant's leaves used as an herb, and coriander refers to the seeds used as a spice.

Either you love cilantro, or you hate it. Many people say it tastes like soap to them. This is believed to be caused by aldehyde in soaps, which is found naturally in cilantro. However, if you do love it, this plant is a great choice for your vertical garden! It is fast-growing, aromatic, and prefers cooler temperatures, just like chives.

This plant loves light but shouldn't be grown during high temperatures as it will bolt (meaning it produces a flowering stem before harvest and the leaves are usually bitter and not good for consumption). You can place this plant in a spot in your vertical garden that gets enough light during the day but is also shaded.

- Plant the seeds about a quarter of an inch into the soil, spaced 1 to 2 inches apart.
- Keep the seeds moist during their germination and sow them every three weeks.
- Once the plant is established, it won't require as much water, so be careful not to overwater it.

Dill

https://pixabay.com/es/photos/eneldo-especia-planta-alimentos-2826179/

Dill might not be in everyone's pantries, but it's a great addition to soups and stews and is used in pickling. It is an easy plant to grow. It likes soil temperature to be around 65° F. Once planted, seedlings should appear quickly, in just under two weeks. If you want a constant supply of dill, you may plant it every couple of weeks or allow it to flower and bolt so that its seeds spread, and you'll have more the following year.

- Plant the seeds about a quarter of an inch into the soil, spaced 18 inches apart.
- Place its container in full sun with well-draining soil that is rich in organic matter.
- When you start seeing seedlings, thin the plants to about 15 inches apart if they aren't already like that.
- Keep the soil moist and water it abundantly when growing the plant.

Lavender

https://pxhere.com/en/photo/660094

Lavender is one of the most versatile plants and is used for eating, cleaning, or décor. It has the most beautiful scent and will look beautiful any time of the year in your home. Another benefit is that it attracts butterflies and bees, which will help pollinate your garden.

Even though this plant has amazing benefits, not only for your garden but in your home as well, it may not be the easiest to plant, so you should consider buying starter plants instead of seeds. They are an easy plant when it comes to soil, as they thrive in most soil types, even a dense one like clay. Just make sure you add organic matter if you intend to use a compacted soil to improve drainage, as lavender doesn't like a lot of moisture. In fact, its roots will rot easily if there is excess moisture, so be careful even when watering them.

- Plant it two to three feet apart.
- Use mulch to keep weeds away but be careful with the excess moisture mulch can bring to the plant's crown, as it'll create root rot.
- Water it once or twice a week until the plant is established, and then only every two to three weeks. Once you see its buds formed, go back to watering it once or twice a week.
- If you live in a region that experiences severe cold during winter, consider moving the plants indoors where it has a lot of light but is protected from the harsh weather. A modular system would be great for this plant.

Marjoram

https://pixabay.com/es/photos/mejorana-cocinando-2370814/

You can use marjoram in most of your dishes as a seasoning. It also works great in any meat dish. It has a very mild flavor, so don't be afraid to test it out. This plant likes light and well-draining soil. If you want it ready for spring, you can start its growth indoors in early spring or late winter. Soak the seeds overnight and then sow them into potting soil. Once they are established, you can transplant the seedlings outside when the temperatures rise.

- Plant the seeds about 12 inches apart.
- Water them regularly, making sure to add nutrients to them occasionally to maximize growth.
- To generate new growth, prune it to close to the soil. Do this once flower buds appear, indicating the end of the harvesting period.

Mint

https://pixabay.com/es/photos/hierba-menta-cortar-aislado-planta-2540568/

Who doesn't love mint? It's favored by many people because this plant smells incredible and makes a great herb for many dishes and even cocktails. Growing it is easy. Some may even say too easy, as it will completely take over your other plants. Planting mint is great, but you should isolate it from other plants.

This plant loves light, well-drained soil and will tolerate some shade. You can plant mint near tomatoes, but not in the same container because they take over the tomato plant. In colder temperatures, either bring the container inside or cover it to protect the plant.

- Plant them 2 feet apart.
- Keep the soil moist but use a light mulch to keep the leaves clean.
- Prune them generously and often. If they are controlled in a container, you shouldn't have an issue. Be aware that they are easily pulled out since they are shallow-rooted.

Oregano

https://pxhere.com/en/photo/721607

You cannot think of Italy or pizza without thinking of oregano; one does not exist without the other. This plant is very versatile as an herb, and it's an excellent ground cover, even when using it in your vertical garden. You'll want to keep it somewhere sunny and only plant it when the temperature rises. Like the other plants, you can plant it indoors and then transfer it outside when it gets warmer.

This plant is not difficult to grow, so you can plant seeds or use a cutting from an established plant. You can grow it in the same container as any other vegetable, as oregano is a good companion plant and won't take over others.

- Plant the seeds 8 to 10 inches apart.
- Use well-draining soil and water it thoroughly but less often – touch the soil to see if it's dry; only water it if it is.
- Trim it regularly to increase growth and branching.
- You can harvest the leaves as you need them, but the most flavorful ones are found right before the flowers bloom.

Parsley

https://pxhere.com/en/photo/492889

Parsley is from the same family as dill, but possibly a lot more common in our kitchens. This herb goes well with fewer dishes as it can have a strong flavor, but it will pair beautifully with plain white rice. One of its biggest advantages is that it's rich in iron and vitamins A and C, so use it abundantly in your cooking.

This plant loves the sun and needs to get about six to eight hours of it every day. A nutrient-rich and well-draining soil is the best for parsley.

You'll know it's ready to harvest when the leaf stems have three segments. Always cut the outer leaves, and the inner ones will continue to mature. To speed up its growth, you may want to start planting it indoors about eight weeks before the last spring frost. You can then move them outside about four weeks later.

- Plant the seeds about a quarter of an inch into the soil, spaced 6 to 8 inches apart.

- Keep the soil moist at all times while the seeds germinate – it will take some time for you to see seedlings, but be patient; they will appear.

- If the temperature gets too high, water it abundantly and add mulch to help keep the soil moist.

Rosemary

https://pixabay.com/es/photos/rama-romero-flor-especias-azul-1525050/

Rosemary is such a beautiful herb to keep in your pantry; it adds flavor to your lamb, stews, and any type of grilled fish. You can do so much with a simple branch, and if you grow it in your vertical garden, it will likely remain green all year round. This is an easy plant to grow.

However, it may be difficult to grow from seed, so, if you can, buy a starter plant to put into one of your containers.

This plant loves the sun, well-draining soil, and space. Trim it often, as rosemary can spread about four feet in all directions, so keeping it contained is important for your vertical garden. Don't over-water it, as rosemary does not like to be consistently wet.

- Sow the seeds or starter plant in well-draining soil. If the temperatures are lower than 70° F, consider bringing your container indoors or plant it later in the year when the temperatures have risen.
- Water it regularly but be careful not to overwater it – this plant does not like being wet. If your vertical garden is layered, consider placing it in the top row.
- When grown, you can cut off the stems and dry them in your kitchen by hanging them.

Sage

https://pixabay.com/es/photos/sabio-hierbas-hierbas-culinarias-1544884/

According to some myths, if you want to do well in business, you need to grow sage in your garden. If you don't use this herb in the kitchen often, that may be a good reason for growing it. This plant blooms the prettiest flowers in different colors and if you want the edible variety, consider planting the variety called Salvia officinalis, as this is the one most commonly used in the kitchen.

Sage likes full sun exposure and well-draining soil. It doesn't like being overwatered when it's established, just like rosemary, so be careful not to water it if the soil is still moist. Also, like rosemary, it is easier to grow from a starter plant.

- Plant the seeds 2 feet apart in well-drained soil. You can sow them two weeks before the last spring frost for a head start.
- Water the plant regularly while it's still growing to avoid it drying out. Once established, check the soil moisture before watering it.
- Prune it every year for a more active plant and replace it every few years.

Tarragon

https://pixabay.com/es/photos/estrag%C3%B3n-planta-hierbas-culinarias-115368/

Tarragon, especially French tarragon, is a great herb to pair with meats and seafood. It's a beautiful green plant with a lot of texture that will look great in your vertical garden. Tarragon must be planted as a cutting from an established plant, which you can then transplant into your own vertical garden.

- Plant the established plants two feet apart in well-drained soil.
- Water them regularly and use mulch if the temperature is very low during fall and winter.
- Prune them often to avoid flowering.

Thyme

https://pixabay.com/es/photos/tomillo-hierba-medicinal-cocinero-2854035/

Thyme is such a fun plant. It's unique-looking and adds a beautiful, new shade of green to any vertical garden. Its usage in the kitchen is well known, and it can even help you get rid of insects!

Even though this plant is versatile and tastes delicious in most recipes, it does not grow very well from seeds. This means you're better off buying a starter plant for your vertical garden. It loves full sun exposure and heat and does not like to be wet, like rosemary. So be careful not to overwater it.

- Plant your young plant when the temperature is above 70° F.
- Make sure the soil is draining well so that your plant is not wet at all times, and only water it again when the soil is fully dry.
- Grow it near rosemary as they have similar needs.
- Prune it once or twice a year to contain its growth.

The table below shows you the different types of plants discussed and a summary of their properties:

Herb	Sun Exposure	Soil Type	Soil pH	Bloom
Basil	Full sun	Loamy	Slightly Acidic to Neutral	Summer
Chives	Full sun	Loamy, sandy	Slightly Acidic to Neutral	Summer
Cilantro	Full sun, Part sun	Loamy	Neutral	Spring
Dill	Full sun	Loamy, sandy	Slightly Acidic to Neutral	Summer
Lavender	Full sun		Neutral to Alkaline	Summer
Marjoram	Full sun	Loamy	Neutral	

Herb	Sun Exposure	Soil Type	Soil pH	Bloom
Mint	Full sun	Loamy	Neutral	
Oregano	Full sun	Loamy	Neutral	Summer
Parsley	Full sun, Part sun	Loamy, sandy	Slightly Acidic to Neutral	
Rosemary	Full sun	Loamy, sandy	Slightly Acidic to Neutral	Summer
Sage	Full sun	Loamy, sandy	Slightly Acidic to Neutral	Summer
Tarragon	Full sun, Part sun	Loamy, sandy	Slightly Acidic to Neutral	
Thyme	Full sun, Part sun	Loamy, sandy	Alkaline	

For the best results, consult the table above and match herbs that work well together and require similar care or have similar growth patterns. This will make it easier for you as a beginner; however, if you truly love a variety of different plants, go ahead. Plant it, anyway! Remember my first tip; you have to love them. It's your vertical garden and your decision, so just have fun doing it.

The Best Plants for Living Walls

Now that we've covered the best herbs for your living wall, let's look at which non-edible plants are suitable for your space. Maybe you're thinking about what plants work best indoors. Perhaps you live in a windy city, so you need stronger stalks and stems. These are all important considerations when putting together your living wall. In this next section, we will be looking at the best non-edible plants for your living wall.

We'll talk about foliage plants that tolerate darker spots and others that do well in drier soil. We have it all – this is a list that will help you choose the best plants for your space. You may have a lot of sunlight but not a lot of time to water your plants, or more time but not as much light. It's all possible if you plan ahead carefully. Let's look at your options.

In the glossary below, you'll find the best plants for your living wall:

1. Air plants
2. Coleus
3. Croton
4. Elephant Ears
5. English Ivy
6. Hosta
7. Pothos
8. Spider plants

Air plants

https://unsplash.com/photos/green-leafed-plant-on-brown-pot-lOTEL9Vfz7k

This type of plant is part of the bromeliad family and is easily grown without soil. This means it can be a great plant to include in your hydroponic irrigation system if you're installing one. They love light and water but don't do so well if they cannot dry off, so if you're planting them in your living wall, make sure your container and irrigation system is set to let them dry after watering. Good air circulation is important for them, and because they love humidity and moisture, they will work great in your indoor living wall. This is especially true if this wall is near the kitchen or bathroom, as air plants love the moisture in those areas and will thrive on it.

- Don't use soil; use water for these plants.
- Mist them every couple of days or drown them in room-temperature water for half an hour every week and a half. Let them dry well before placing them on your living wall again.
- Trim dead leaves – if you find brown spots, you need to water them more often or move them around your living wall for a better spot.

Coleus

https://pixabay.com/es/photos/coleo-flor-jard%C3%ADn-de-flores-p%C3%A9talos-4291118/

There are more than six hundred varieties of this plant, so you have most likely seen at least one type. This plant is a great addition to your living wall, no matter which variety you end up choosing, as it will add color, texture, and grandeur to your space. It is an amazingly easy, low-maintenance plant, so it's perfect for beginners. Certain varieties do very well in semi-shade, in case your living wall happens to be in a darker room. For semi-shade type of coleus, you can choose "Brilliancy," "Fishnet Stockings," "Mardi gras," or even "Japanese Giant" – make sure to ask around in your garden center if you need help finding the right variety.

- Sow the seeds about ten weeks before the last frost date. If you're planting this outdoors, make sure the temperature is higher than the normal winter temperature before moving it outside.
- Choose well-draining soil and a spot that is protected from the wind.
- Water it well and keep it moist for the first week after planting.
- If the topsoil is dry, you can water it again.

Croton

https://pixabay.com/es/photos/planta-de-croton-vibrante-jard%C3%ADn-2071620/

Croton is a stunning plant with shades of green, scarlet, orange, and even a few yellows thrown in the mix. It's a bushy plant and has an incredibly eye-catching texture. If you plan to grow Croton in your home, you shouldn't allow pets or children near it, as it is poisonous, including the seeds. On the other hand, croton will be a lovely addition to your living wall as it will add more depth and texture.

- Sow the seeds in well-draining soil when the temperature is over 65° F. Use a container that is large and heavy because this plant is heavy.
- Water it lightly from time to time – moisture is fine, but not wet soil.

- Croton needs sunlight, so only consider if your indoor spot has enough light during the day.
- Trim it to your liking and to prevent it from tipping over plants that are below.

Elephant Ears

Elephant ears need to be part of your living wall! They have gorgeous heart-shaped leaves with prominent veins running through them, and their color range goes from lime green to almost black. They come from tropical Asia, so they prefer moist soils and not a lot of sunlight. Once established, elephant ears get large, so make sure you trim them often and consider placing them at the bottom of your living wall.

- Plant the tuber one inch below wet soil.
- Fertilize it once a month.
- Water it at its base, so you don't get water on its leaves. Don't let the soil dry out, as the plant will struggle to survive.
- Remove brown leaves by cutting them as close to the tuber as possible.

English Ivy

https://pixabay.com/es/photos/hiedra-hiedra-inglesa-plantas-verde-5904224/

Ivies are a must in any living wall. They're climbing plants, and they add a magical touch to any home. English ivy leaves are small and may vary in shape. They are not on the bushier side, but they will help cover up a few empty spots you may have in between other bigger plants. This plant would also be great in a trellis as it's very flexible and easily weaves around any frame.

- Plant it in well-draining soil.
- English Ivy needs light but not direct sunlight - if your home is too warm, it may not grow well. It needs cooler temperatures.
- Water it regularly, but only when the soil is dry to the touch.
- Trim it as needed.

Hosta

https://pixabay.com/es/photos/lirio-de-pl%C3%A1tano-hosta-1579042/

Hostas are an incredibly eclectic plant that can range from small varieties to ones three feet tall. This plant also has leaf colors in white, blue-green, and lime green, and they may be smooth or have ridges. Have your pick! Whichever variety you choose, though, hosta are breathtaking. They can also attract pollinators if your living wall is outdoors, and they bloom in summer – their flowers are also colorful!

- Place the plant's roots in well-draining soil, leaving its crown visible at the soil surface.
- Add fertilizer after planting it and use a mulch to keep it moist.
- Water it regularly – hosta need soil that is moist but not wet.
- Cut its flower stalks to encourage new growth.

Pothos

https://pixabay.com/es/photos/planta-pothos-epipremnum-aureum-3816945/

Pothos is a beginner's best friend. It won't die if it's exposed to too much or too little light. It will also tolerate too much water or too little water. Even the soil type won't affect it negatively. You will love it for how easy it will be on you. This plant is a great one for your indoor living wall as its requirements are very low, that's why it's sometimes called "Devil's Ivy": it just keeps coming back to life! On that note, be careful if you have pets or children, as this plant is poisonous.

- Plant the seeds in well-draining soil – they do not tolerate wet soil.

- Put it in a large container. If it's inside, room temperature is perfect for optimal growth. Pothos like light – but not direct sunlight.
- Water it once the soil is dry.
- Fertilize it about once a month in spring and summer.
- Trim it as needed. If it starts browning, remove those leaves and stems immediately.

Spider Plants

Mokkie, CC BY-SA 3.0 <https://creativecommons.org/licenses/by-sa/3.0>, via Wikimedia Commons https://commons.wikimedia.org/wiki/File:Spider_Plant_(Chlorophytum_comosum).jpg

Spider plants are a very popular type of plant in homes because they possess a unique shade of green. They have long, thin foliage that is light green with a white line running along the center. They may bloom in summer with white flowers. They also have an air-purifying ability. It won't truly work if you only own one or two, but it's a good fact to throw in when describing your living wall.

- Sow the seeds in well-draining soil.
- Keep the plant in a bright place but away from direct sunlight.
- Water it once a week, and once fully established, water it two to three times a week, never letting its soil dry out.

- Fertilize it once a month during spring and summer.

The table below shows you the different types of plants discussed and a summary of their properties:

Plant	Sun Exposure	Soil Type	Soil pH	Bloom
Air plant	Full sun but no direct sunlight	N/A	N/A	Varies
Coleus	Full sun, Partial sun	Any	Neutral	Summer
Croton	Full sun, Partial sun	Loamy	Neutral	Varies
Elephant Ears	Part sun	Any	Neutral to Slightly Alkaline	
English Ivy	Partial sun, Shade	Loamy, sandy	Loamy, sandy	
Hosta	Shade	Loamy	Neutral	Summer
Pothos	Partial sun	Loamy, sandy	Neutral	
Spider plant	Partial sun, Shade	Loamy	Neutral	Summer, Fall, Spring

For the best results, consult the table above and match plants that work well together and require similar care or have similar growth patterns. Remember to create a fun wall to look at as you'll want to spend a lot of your time here, and others will want to spend their time relaxing next to it.

If you opt for a full hydroponic system, then remember to set it up so that each plant gets its specific watering needs met. You should also use modular containers, if possible, so you have the option of moving things around if a particular plant is not loving its spot.

In the next chapter, we'll look at what fruits you should grow in your vertical garden if you want to grow something edible and sweet.

Chapter 7: Fruit Trees for Your Vertical Garden

Imagine walking out into your backyard on a hot, sunny day, ready to water your plants, only to see a special surprise! Your first homegrown strawberry. Or maybe it's a tomato. What's important is that you can have this experience yourself. Growing your own fruit may be the smartest decision ever. You'll have an unlimited supply of fresh fruit that you grew in your very own balcony or backyard, just a few steps away. The pride that also comes from growing your own fruit is just the cherry on top of the cake.

Many types of fruit offer an excellent opportunity to dive into your new passion for gardening as many of them are very easy plants to grow. Climbing fruit plants will make it even easier for you because they thrive on vertical supports like trellises. You won't need to worry about using up what little space you have, and you'll be enjoying your vertical garden in more ways than by just looking at it. It'll become a part of your meals and family traditions.

You'll have to consider choosing the perfect location for these crops as most of them require at least half a day of sunlight. Some of them might do well in more shaded areas, but the disadvantage there is they'll yield less fruit. The soil you use is also important to think about since, for most fruits, a combination of sandy and loamy soils is ideal.

We'll discuss this further in this chapter when we look at the best fruits to grow in your vertical garden and give you the information you need to plant each of them.

Below, you'll find a list of the best fruits to grow in your vertical garden:

1. Blackberries
2. Blueberries
3. Cucumbers
4. Grapes
5. Kiwifruit
6. Melons
7. Raspberries
8. Strawberries
9. Tomatoes
10. Watermelon

Blackberries

Photo by Pixabay: https://www.pexels.com/photo/berries-blackberries-blur-close-up-134581/

Blackberries are one of the best fruits to grow in your vertical garden. They're easy to grow, and they're delicious! Once established, you may expect to have a great harvest every few days. The trailing kind has canes that need to be attached to a trellis for support, which makes them perfect for your vertical garden as you'll already have the support they need.

This fruit is perennial, meaning its root will survive, but its canes will die after they've borne fruit, so you'll need to prune them for new ones to grow. Wait for the temperature to rise before planting them, as doing so too early may kill the plant. If you're reading this and counting on having blackberries in just a few months, you may be disappointed to learn that they only bear fruit in the second year. If you're looking forward to harvesting this fruit, you should be aware of this rather long wait.

- Plant them no more than one inch deep in well-draining soil and water them thoroughly.
- Use a trellis or vertical support to attach all canes once they've been established.
- Use mulch all year round to help prevent weeds and retain moisture.
- Water them two to three times per week, making sure they get a total of one inch of water weekly.
- Prune canes once they've died and turned black near the soil.

Blueberries

Comfreak, CC0, via Wikimedia Commons
https://commons.wikimedia.org/wiki/File:Wet_blueberries_close_up.jpg

Blueberries are also one of the easiest fruits to grow on your balcony, backyard, or garden. They have so many health benefits that you'll be missing out if you don't include them in your vertical garden. Blueberries are full of antioxidants and have vitamins C, K, and the mineral manganese. They are said to help lower blood pressure, improve memory, and reduce LDL cholesterol levels. This means that they're not only tasty but also packed with vitamins that will improve your health.

This plant likes the sunlight and needs to be protected from wind and birds who just love to eat them! They can be grown in a container, which is ideal because blueberries require acidic soil – a type that is easily mixed or found, though, so don't worry. Like blackberries, you'll have to wait to enjoy your crops as the plant doesn't bear fruit until its second year.

The best varieties to grow in containers are "Top Hat," "Pink Lemonade," and "Pink Champagne."

- Plant the blueberry bush in a well-draining, acidic soil just below the surface. Add peat moss to your soil a few months before planting to ensure it's acidic enough for optimal development. Water it thoroughly.
- Place the container in a nice, sunny spot where it's also sheltered from the wind and birds.
- Fertilize it one month after planting.
- Use mulch to retain moisture but leave the trunk of the bush clear for proper airflow.
- Water it regularly so that it receives up to two inches of water weekly.
- Prune it after about four years to stimulate growth (pruning is not needed before then).

Cucumbers

https://www.pickpik.com/cucumber-salad-food-healthy-green-fresh-3088

This might be surprising to hear, but cucumbers are actually fruits and not vegetables, as they grow from flowers and contain seeds. This fruit is ideally grown on a trellis, so it will be easier to harvest. Growing it on a trellis also reduces the likelihood of fungal diseases and pests.

Cucumbers love sun and water, and they will grow easily in the right conditions. Pick them regularly so as to not weigh down the plant. Another reason to pick them sooner rather than later is that they won't taste as sweet once they are large.

Vining cucumbers are the ones you should be looking for, as they are the most suited for climbing up a trellis or vertical structure. They also grow really fast, in just a few weeks. If you want to cut them to eat, pick them when they're 6 to 8 inches long, and if you want to pickle them, harvest them when they're at two inches.

- Sow seeds one inch deep into a well-draining soil rich in nutrients. You can mix in your compost before planting them.
- Place your container somewhere with full sun exposure.

- Water it regularly, as cucumbers love water – one inch per week. Using a drip irrigation system will help not to get the leaves wet. Once fruits begin forming, increase the amount of water to one gallon per week.
- Pick the fruits using a knife or clippers, cutting the stem just above the fruit. Pick them often; if you don't, the plants will stop producing fruit.

Grapes

https://unsplash.com/photos/person-showing-blue-berries-i5Crg4KLblY

Grapes are so versatile as a fruit that there's no way not to love them. They are an investment because they take their time to establish and require quite a bit of care, but if you love them, they will give your vertical garden a dramatic cascading effect of beautiful vines. Moreover, if taken care of properly, this plant may last for about thirty years!

Grapes love the sun and need to have good airflow. It may take three years for them to start bearing fruit, but the wait will be worth it.

- Soak the grape vine's roots in water for about three hours before planting.

- Plant grape vines in well-draining soil in an area with full sun exposure. Water it thoroughly.
- Use mulch to retain water.
- Fertilize lightly only in the second year after planting.
- Prune it when the plant is dormant after the first year. Remove the canes that are already bearing fruit to allow for new growth.

Kiwi

https://pixabay.com/es/photos/kiwi-fruta-comida-nuevo-dieta-400143/

Kiwis are a delicious green fruit that is loved by many. Their vines can grow quite tall, so make sure you have enough space for them before you consider growing this fruit on your small balcony or indoors. Kiwis are a climbing vine, so they are a perfect addition to your vertical structure. If you live in an especially cold area but want to grow your own kiwis, you might still be able to. There are two types of this plant, and the hardy kiwi (also known as the kiwi berry) can tolerate subzero temperatures for limited periods.

If you're looking into growing a more common type of kiwi, then it's the kiwifruit you should go for. They like the sun and warmer temperatures, but you will need a male and female to produce fruit. Just like many other fruits, you'll have to wait a while before enjoying it, but the wait will be worth it.

- Plant kiwi vines in well-draining soil, just deep enough to cover the roots.
- Attach the vines to a strong vertical structure, as they need good support. Keep in mind that the weight of the fruit will break the structure if it is not sturdy enough. Water them thoroughly.
- Place them in a very sunny spot with good airflow.
- Water them regularly, making sure the roots are not consistently wet, as kiwi roots tend to rot easily.
- Fertilize in the spring after their first year.
- Prune the female vines in winter and the male ones after blooming time.
- Harvest the fruits when they are soft to the touch.

Melons

https://www.pickpik.com/watermelon-sweet-juicy-fruit-melon-ripe-2837

Melons are another great option for your vertical garden, even though they are heavy fruit. As with other heavy fruits, you need to ensure your vertical structure will support the weight during fruiting. They are a delicious fruit that is best enjoyed in warmer months and makes anyone with a sweet tooth happy.

This fruit loves the sun and lots of water, so you need to keep it hydrated and in a sunny spot with at least half a day of sunlight. They don't tolerate subzero temperatures but will produce fruit much faster than your berries. Many gardeners use an old t-shirt to support the weight of this fruit while it's growing to avoid any possible damage to its vines.

- Plant melons one inch deep in well-draining soil when the temperatures are no lower than 60° F, and there is no risk of frost.
- Water them regularly with up to 1.5 gallons a week, but make sure their leaves dry off well to avoid any fungal diseases. Once they start fruiting, reduce the amount of water, as melons like hot and dry weather. This should give them a sweet taste.
- Fertilize with a non-heavy nitrogen liquid fertilizer.
- Prune the ends of the vines after fruiting.
- Harvest when their rinds are a hue of yellow or when you find cracks on the stems. If you see them separate themselves from the vine, they are probably overripe; you want to pick them before they reach this point.

Raspberries

ulleo on Pixabay, CC0, via Wikimedia Commons https://commons.wikimedia.org/wiki/File:Close-up_of_raspberries_on_bush.jpg

Raspberries are quite a versatile plant to grow on your balcony or small space as they are self-fertile. This means they only need one bush to produce fruit. Even though raspberries usually prefer colder temperatures, new varieties will allow gardeners to grow them even in hotter climates.

You probably know the summer-fruiting raspberries, as they are more common, but there is another type called "fall-fruiting" or "ever-bearing," which produces fruit in the fall. The summer-fruiting type produces fruit once a year, usually during the summertime, and reutilizes the same canes. However, the ever-bearing type produces berries on new canes, fruiting in fall and sometimes the following summer. They attract pollinators and will produce fruit in the second year like most berries.

- Soak raspberries roots for two hours before planting.
- Plant them in well-draining soil, leaving the crown one inch above the ground.
- Place them in a sunny spot – raspberries may also do well in semi-shade; however, they won't produce as much fruit. If you don't have a sunny spot for them, you may consider a partially sunny spot.

- Use mulch to retain moisture and prevent weeds from appearing.
- Water it regularly – up to one inch a week from spring until harvest.
- Prune its old canes back to the ground (old canes will be the fruiting ones that have brown stems). New, green canes (also called primocanes) will be produced every year, so don't worry about cutting the old ones to the ground as you'll be stimulating new growth.
- Harvest raspberries in early summer after the first year.

Strawberries

https://pixabay.com/es/photos/fresa-rojo-macro-fruta-horizontal-2960534/

Strawberries are one of every gardener's must-haves. They are one of the easiest fruits to grow, kids love them, and they are sweeter when you grow them yourself – not just because you grew them yourself, but because they truly are sweeter right when you pick them. They will also look beautiful on your vertical garden as they spill out of their container, covering up any unnecessary gaps.

They love the sun, and there are three types of strawberries, the most common among home gardeners being the June-bearing ones. These fruit in June, as the name indicates, over about three weeks. Another type is the ever-bearing one, which fruits in the spring and then lightly again in the summer and again in the late summer or early fall. The third type is the day-neutral one, which produces fruits continuously if the temperature is between 35° F and 85° F. However, the harvest is inferior to the June-bearers. Like your other berries, it'll take a year for your plant to start bearing fruit.

- Plant the seeds in well-draining soil, leaving the crown exposed when the temperature is warm.
- Water it thoroughly after planting.
- Use mulch to keep it moist.
- Water it regularly – one inch per square foot per week.
- Cut off blossoms in the first year, as this encourages the plant to develop strong and healthy roots. This will lead to a better harvest in the following year.
- Harvest when ripe, usually about six weeks after blossoming, by cutting by the stem.

Tomatoes

https://unsplash.com/photos/red-tomato-on-brown-tree-branch-qwUtuzm_WzI

Tomatoes are another food that most people consider a vegetable, but they are actually a fruit. Tomatoes are also a great ally to beginners are they are easy to grow, especially in a vertical garden. They love the sun and warm temperatures, and this fruit is an excellent pick for growing indoors if you place it next to a window with plenty of sunlight – they need about eight hours daily. The best thing is that it won't take you a year to see results, as tomatoes usually start bearing fruit around three months after planting, depending on the cultivar.

For a vertical garden, the bush or dwarf variety of tomatoes is the best choice, as they won't need to be staked.

- Sow seeds a quarter of an inch deep into loose, well-draining soil. If it's being planted outside, ensure the temperatures are around (or ideally above) 70° F.
- Add organic matter to your soil a couple of weeks before planting for optimal results.
- Water it generously in the first few days after planting and then about 1.2 gallons per week.
- Use mulch after a few weeks to conserve moisture.
- Fertilize it every three to four weeks, using a slow-release, low-nitrogen fertilizer.
- Harvest when tomatoes are firm to the touch.

Watermelon

https://pxhere.com/en/photo/715932

Watermelons are another popular fruit amongst most people. They can be eaten raw, juiced, used in salads, and much more. Like melons, they have varieties that are suited to be grown vertically, and you may use the same system of an old t-shirt to support their weight if needed. Planting them in a spot with sunlight and good airflow is the best for them, and in just a short couple of months (maybe three), you'll be able to enjoy your first homegrown watermelons!

If you live in a colder area, you may start planting the seeds indoors three weeks before your last frost date. If you live in a warmer place and the temperatures are above 70° F, then grow them outside right away.

- Compost your soil a couple of weeks before planting.
- Plant seeds a quarter of an inch deep into well-draining soil. Use a large container to sow them in.
- Water them regularly with about two inches of water per week until they fruit. Keep the soil moist but try not to wet the leaves. Reduce the amount of water when fruiting.

- When ripening, usually over two weeks, place cardboard or straw underneath the fruit to prevent rotting.
- Harvest when ripe – they won't ripen after being picked. To see if your watermelon is ripe, thump it. If it sounds hollow, then it's good to go! Harvest by cutting by the stems close to the fruit.

The table below shows you the different fruits discussed and a summary of their requirements:

Fruit	Sun Exposure	Soil Type	Soil pH	Plant in (season)
Blackberries	Do well in semi-shade	Sandy	Acidic	Early spring
Blueberries	Do well in semi-shade	Any	Acidic	Spring or late Fall
Cucumbers	Full sun	Loamy	Slightly Acidic to Neutral	Early Spring
Grapes	Full sun	Any	Slightly Acidic to Neutral	Early Spring
Kiwifruit	Full sun	Loamy, sandy	Slightly Acidic to Neutral	Spring

Fruit	Sun Exposure	Soil Type	Soil pH	Plant in (season)
Melons	Full sun	Loamy, sandy	Slightly Acidic to Neutral	Spring
Raspberries	Do well in semi-shade	Any	Slightly Acidic to Neutral	Early Spring
Strawberries	Full sun	Loamy	Slightly Acidic to Neutral	Spring
Tomatoes	Full sun	Loamy	Acidic, Slightly Acidic to Neutral	Spring
Watermelon	Full sun	Sandy	Slightly Acidic to Neutral	Spring

With this information, you will hopefully make the best decision for you and your vertical garden. Remember that care and patience are a gardener's best friends, and without them, you won't see the results you're hoping for. Even if it takes you a year or two to get your delicious fruits, if you put in the work, the wait will be worth it.

If you're not set on specific fruits because they're your favorites, try to use the table above to help you match fruits that work well together and require similar care or have similar growth patterns. This will ensure that you'll have an easier time when first planting your crops. Consider sunlight and watering needs as these will influence your crops the most. Other than that, any fruits you choose to grow will be tasty, and more importantly, they will be grown by you, which will make them extra sweet.

Fruits may not be part of your plan for a vertical garden, but what about vegetables? Going outside and getting a head of lettuce to prepare for dinner is something most people wouldn't know about, but you can do it. In Chapter 8, we'll be talking about the best veggies to plant in your vertical garden.

Chapter 8: Vertical Veggies

Growing your own vegetables is any gardener's dream. Fresh, chemical-free crops that go right to your table are the absolute best way to nourish yourself and your family. Some people believe they can never grow their own veggies because you need tons and tons of space. However, you probably know by now that this is not true. A vertical garden will allow you to feed your family right, all from the comfort of your balcony or small backyard. Growing veggies vertically means you won't have to think twice while you're at the supermarket, making sure you haven't forgotten anything for your favorite dish.

Besides possibly giving you some privacy, a vertical garden filled with vegetables will make your experience more exciting when you're ready to harvest your first-ever crop. Often, they'll be even tastier than your store-bought vegetables, so you have nothing to lose!

Refer to Chapter 4 if you need some ideas on how to DIY your vertical garden using trellises or baskets, or even plastic bottles. As long as you have large containers that will allow your vegetables to grow, you can even plant vine crops. Anything goes once you are knowledgeable and know exactly which steps you need to take to be successful.

In this chapter, we'll be looking at the best vegetables and greens to grow in your vertical garden, their characteristics, and how they should be planted. This should give you the information you need to choose the most suitable plants for your garden.

Here's a list of the best vegetables and greens to grow in your vertical garden:

1. Beans
2. Cabbage
3. Carrots
4. Garlic
5. Lettuce
6. Onions
7. Peas
8. Peppers
9. Radishes
10. Spinach

Beans

https://pixabay.com/es/photos/frijoles-vegetal-cosecha-nuevo-3702999/

Beans are a staple in many households, so it shouldn't surprise you that they are loved and very commonly grown by gardeners. Beans are also one of the easiest plants to grow, so as a first-time gardener, you should be happy with them.

There are two types of beans: bush beans and pole beans. There are a few differences between them, and some say pole beans taste better. Bush beans might be your initial choice because they are very compact. Pole beans would be ideal for a vertical structure since they grow as climbing vines. They are also more disease-resistant, and they grow in about a month, so you don't need a lot of patience to see results.

- Sow the seeds one inch deep into well-draining soil. This should be done outdoors when the temperature is above 50° F. Use a trellis as support for the climbing vines.
- Water them regularly – about two inches of water per week. Pole beans like water, but make sure their foliage dries well after watering.
- Add mulch to the soil the keep moisture in.
- Harvest every day to encourage more growth. They should be harvested while they're still young and tender.

Cabbage

https://pixabay.com/es/photos/col-de-col-rizada-verduras-3860933/

Cabbage is a well-loved and popular vegetable. Packed with vitamins, it can be added to salads, soups, or eaten with meats and bread. It's a well-rounded veggie and an easy one to grow if you provide it with the right conditions.

Cabbages do not like hot climates, so you'll have to wait for the temperature to drop to plant it. Depending on where you live, this may be around the late summertime. Making sure the soil temperature is right will make growing cabbages much easier.

- Prepare the soil by mixing it with compost a couple of weeks before planting.
- Sow the seeds 12 to 24 inches apart in well-draining soil.
- Water it regularly with up to two inches of water per week.
- If the temperatures drop below 45° F, you should consider covering them.
- Fertilize your crops after two weeks. You may also add a nitrogen fertilizer a week later.
- Harvest by cutting at the base of its head, then remove the stem and root from the soil to prevent disease.

Carrots

Yerson Retamel, CC0, via Wikimedia Commons
https://commons.wikimedia.org/wiki/File:Fresh_Carrots.jpg

Carrots are also part of the family of vegetables that enjoy cooler temperatures, and they don't even mind frost. They like their soil to be loose and sandy (or loamy), and you can plant them during spring or late summer. They will take about 3 to 4 months to be ready for harvest and three weeks to germinate, so you'll need to be patient with this vegetable.

This vegetable is well-loved because it can be grown in many climates and gives you a choice between a summer or fall harvest.

- Make sure your soil is loose; no clumps should be in the way of your carrots' roots.
- Add used coffee grounds to the soil before planting.
- Sow seeds a quarter of an inch deep, four weeks before the last spring frost date for a summer harvest or ten weeks before the first fall frost for a fall harvest.
- Water it frequently. It should get one inch of water per week at the beginning and two inches once the roots start to mature.
- Use mulch to retain moisture and to protect the roots from sunlight.
- Harvest when the size is to your liking.

Garlic

https://unsplash.com/photos/a-couple-of-garlics-sitting-on-top-of-a-table-8NJKVefiB6s

You'll be happy to know that this very popular ingredient is easy to grow, and you can get started as early as September. Garlic does not like hot weather, so you'll need to plant it before the ground freezes to be able to harvest it in the summertime. It needs low temperatures, around 40° F to grow well.

- Prepare your soil by adding compost to it before planting.
- Plant cloves two inches deep, in their upright position, in well-draining soil.
- Use mulch right up to the last frost date.
- Fertilize it in early spring and again around early May. Use a nitrogen-heavy fertilizer.
- Water it frequently – every 3 to 5 days right until June.
- Harvest by digging up the bulbs using a garden fork.

Lettuce

https://pixabay.com/es/photos/lechuga-lechuga-romana-verduras-2468495/

Lettuce is the ultimate vertical gardener's best friend. Not only will it grow quickly, but it also won't require a lot of care. Imagine getting a fresh head of lettuce from your balcony and quickly throwing together a delicious mixed salad. Plus, lettuce likes the cooler seasons, so you can start planting it even before the first frost. It loves water, so you need to keep it hydrated, but other than that, it's an excellent choice for your vertical garden.

- Prepare the soil by mixing in the organic matter about a week before planting.
- Sow the seeds a quarter of an inch deep in well-draining soil.
- Water it well after planting. Place garlic rows in between lettuce to prevent pests.
- Fertilize it about three weeks after planting.
- Water it regularly – lettuce likes its soil moist but not wet.
- Use organic mulch to help retain moisture and keep the soil temperature cool.
- Harvest heads when they've reached their full size but before maturity.

Onions

https://freerangestock.com/photos/88717/photo-details.html

Another crop that is perfect for the colder months is the onion. Onions are versatile, and you can use them in any dish you can think of. They can also be eaten raw or cooked and even taste excellent when pickled. They are truly magnificent vegetables! They don't require a lot to grow, and you may be surprised by how quickly you'll be making dinners with your own onions.

It is advised to plant onion sets and not seeds because it is much easier to start with the onion bulbs. In just under four months, you'll see full-sized bulbs. They even tolerate frost!

- Prepare the soil by mixing compost in before planting.
- Plant onion sets one inch deep, with the pointed end up, in well-drained, loose soil.
- Fertilize them every few weeks with a nitrogen-heavy fertilizer.
- Add mulch when the bulbs start to develop.
- Water them regularly – about one inch per week.
- When you see brown on their foliage, pull the onions carefully – they'll be ready to harvest.

Peas

https://www.pexels.com/sv-se/foto/artor-artskida-farsk-gron-40788/

Peas are also an incredibly easy vegetable to grow, and planting them yourself will change your view of them forever. Store-bought peas have nothing on the homegrown ones! They taste much better and are suited to growing vertically. Children may even join in the fun and help to plant them! Peas like the sun and an airy spot.

You can choose from one of these three varieties that are perfect to use in meals: sweet peas, snow peas, or snap peas. For the climbing variety, great for your vertical garden, you can choose between snap peas or snow peas. Peas should be planted when the weather is still cool, around March or April.

- Prepare the soil by mixing in compost and mulch around the Fall.
- Sow the seeds 4 to 6 weeks before the last spring frost date, when the temperature is around 60° F.
- Water them sporadically – up to one inch of water per week.
- Peas don't need much fertilizer; however, always choose a fertilizer low in nitrogen if using one.
- Harvesting will be possible in just over a month. Pick them in the morning, gently holding the vine while pulling the pods.

Peppers

https://pixabay.com/es/vectors/pimienta-pimiento-vegetal-comida-154377/

Peppers are an amazing ingredient to have in your kitchen, and they provide a lot of vitamins that we need to stay healthy. Growing them in your vertical garden will also add lots of color to it when they're maturing. They are very resistant to pests and prefer warmer temperatures. You'll have to be a little patient as they may take almost three months to be ready for harvest, but the wait will be worth it.

- Get a head start by sowing the seeds indoors ten weeks before the last spring frost date.
- Sow seeds in well-draining soil rich in organic matter.
- Transfer plants outside when the temperatures are above 65° F. Cover the soil with plastic before transferring to ensure the soil is warm enough.
- Water them regularly – up to two inches of water per week. If the weather is warm, water them every day and cover them with mulch to lower the soil's temperature and keep moisture in.
- Harvest peppers to your liking – remember they can be green, yellow, or red, depending on maturity levels. Red peppers are the sweetest ones.

Radishes

https://pixabay.com/es/photos/r%C3%A1bano-vegetal-ra%C3%ADz-ensalada-1537141/

Radishes are one of the easiest vegetables to grow. They're small and a great vegetable for your vertical garden. You'll see results in no time, so they are a great vegetable for first-time gardeners who need a little extra motivation initially. You can start enjoying your radishes in just three weeks, how great is that!

They don't love hot climates, so they should be planted in spring, but they need light to grow well and become tasty. They need loose soil to allow space for the roots to develop, so you can consider mixing sand in your soil to adjust it as needed.

- Prepare the soil by mixing organic matter into it once the soil is workable.
- Sow seeds a few weeks before the last frost in well-draining, loose soil.
- Water them consistently – moisture is good, but the soil shouldn't be overly wet.
- Harvest when their roots are one inch in diameter at the soil's surface.

Spinach

https://www.pickpik.com/spinach-plant-nutrition-eat-frisch-healthy-132437

This vegetable is rich in essential vitamins like A, B, and C, as well as iron, making it important in our diet. Spinach is very similar to lettuce in terms of growth requirements and can be planted in early spring, sometimes even in winter. Spinach likes cool weather and grows better if given a few weeks of that. Keep in mind that germination will not be successful if the soil is warmer than 70° F.

Spinach likes sunlight, and because its seeds are difficult to transplant, you should plant it in its home right from the start. However, due to its growing requirements, you can start as early as the fall if where you live does not have very cold winters. If the temperature drops, you may consider covering it.

- Prepare the soil by mixing compost into it a week before planting.
- Plant seeds half an inch deep, covering them lightly with well-draining soil.
- Water them thoroughly after planting and continue to water them regularly afterward.
- Use mulch to retain moisture.
- Fertilizing spinach is not necessary.
- Harvest when spinach leaves have reached your preferred size.

Refer to the table below to find a compact list of these vegetables' requirements for optimal growth:

Veggie or Green	Sun Exposure	Soil Type	Soil pH
Beans	Full sun	Any	Neutral
Cabbage	Full sun	Loamy	Neutral
Carrots	Part sun	Loamy, sandy	Neutral
Garlic	Full sun	Loamy, sandy, clay	Neutral
Lettuce	Full sun, Part sun	Loamy, sandy	Neutral
Onions	Full sun	Any	Slightly Acidic to Neutral
Peas	Full sun, Part sun	Loamy, sandy	Slightly Acidic to Neutral
Peppers	Full sun	Loamy	Slightly Acidic to Neutral
Radishes	Full sun, Part sun	Sandy	Neutral
Spinach	Full sun, Part sun	Sandy	Neutral to Slightly Alkaline

Now you have the knowledge you need to make the best decision in terms of what vegetables to include in your vertical garden. Imagine how happy you'll be when you see your first crop turn into your next meal. They may need time and a few adjustments, but that will not stop you.

If you don't have time to grow vegetables or you are not particularly fond of them, then the next chapter may have the answers you've been looking for. A green wall does not have to be just green, it can be as colorful as you'd like, and growing flowers on a living wall just makes it more fun. Read the next chapter to find out more about how to grow flowers on a living wall.

Chapter 9: Growing Flowers on a Living Wall

If you don't feel the need to grow your own crops, it doesn't mean that a vertical garden or living wall isn't for you. As we've seen , you can choose a green wall where none of your plants are edible. You can go for a little more color and add flowers to your vertical space. Flowers can create such a statement out of any blank wall or space in your home, both indoors and outdoors. They catch everyone's attention, and the scents they release may just fill your home with the most natural perfumes.

You can choose flowers that are perennials for a year-round colorful wall. However, if you feel like switching things up, you can always switch containers. Modular containers would be particularly good in this scenario as you can change them regularly or even have others ready for different seasons. It's completely up to you to decide what works best in your space and home. Colors, scents, practicality, and ease of watering are all things to consider when creating your very own living wall.

In this chapter, you'll find information related to the best flowers for a living wall or vertical garden, their characteristics, and their requirements.

This is a list of the best flowers and greens to plant in your vertical garden or living wall:

1. Aurina, or Basket of Gold
2. Clematis
3. Climbing Hydrangea
4. Climbing Rose
5. Creeping Phlox
6. Snow-in-Summer
7. Trumpet Vine
8. Wisteria

Perennials are defined as any plant that lives for more than two years. They are traditionally lower maintenance than annuals, but they do have their requirements to thrive. Keep reading to learn how to grow your perennials in your garden!

Aurinia, or Basket of Gold

https://pixabay.com/sv/photos/sten-sten-%C3%B6rt-aurinia-5175112/

This flower has a stunning yellow color and blooms in spring. It has beautiful gray/blue/green foliage for the rest of the year. It's a low-growing perennial that will cascade down your living wall.

Aurinia is drought resistant, loves the sun, and attracts pollinators. It is very easy to maintain this type of flower, and it'll do well even if you don't do much to it – just leave it be, and it'll look great.

- Plant seeds in well-draining soil. Water well after planting.
- Place it in a sunny spot with some daily shade and water it once a week.
- Fertilize it every few weeks.
- Shear it after flowering for a better-looking result.

Clematis

https://pixabay.com/es/photos/clem%C3%A1tide-planta-trepadora-cerrar-5205114/

This flower is also an easy one to maintain. It has many varieties with different colors, so you can choose whichever one you think will look best on your living wall. They are considered a vining, climbing plant, but they will cascade down when placed on the top row of your wall.

Most of its varieties bloom in the early spring and again in the fall.

Clematis like sunlight and nutrient-rich soil. You'll need to place it somewhere it will get proper air circulation.

- Prepare the soil by adding compost to it before planting.
- Sow the seeds in well-draining soil.
- Water it regularly with one inch of water per week.
- Use mulch to retain moisture and keep the soil cool.
- Prune clematis once a year for a neat appearance.

Climbing Hydrangea

https://pixabay.com/es/photos/hortensia-trepadora-hortensia-flor-1443570/

This flower needs a little more patience to reach its full potential, as it may take from two to five years to reach maturity. Once it does, it's a breathtaking sight. It's a bushy flower with dark green leaves and beautiful, delicate white flowers that bloom in the spring and summertime. They also produce an incredible scent when blooming and, in the fall, the flower heads turn a beautiful red/brown color that suits the season so well.

Climbing hydrangeas prefer partial shade. They may tolerate some sun exposure, but they'll need to be watered more often if that's the case.

- Prepare the soil by adding compost before planting.
- Sow seeds one inch deep into well-draining soil.

- Water them with at least one inch of water per week – climbing hydrangeas like their soil moist but not overly wet. If the temperature rises, water more often.
- Apply mulch to help retain moisture.
- Fertilize them once in the spring before blooming.

Climbing Rose

https://pixabay.com/es/photos/rosa-trepadora-naturaleza-flor-rosa-4891847/

There's nothing wrong with choosing a more common yet beloved flower for your vertical structure. Roses are timeless, and climbing roses are stunning flowers that will be admired all year long. There are plenty of varieties to choose from: hybrid tea roses, bourbons, English roses, and more. Choose your favorite, and you'll have a flower on your living wall that will last for years.

- Plant seeds in well-draining soil.
- Water them regularly – daily when the weather is hot.
- Apply mulch in the Fall.
- Fertilize them in the Spring.

- They'll need pruning after a few years after planting.

Creeping Phlox

https://pixabay.com/es/photos/creeping-phlox-moss-phlox-moss-pink-3894123/

This flower is a beautiful, carpet-like perennial with five-pointed flowers which come in many different colors. It's a cascading type of flower, so it will cover up any spaces you have in your living wall. It's an easy flower to grow as it doesn't require a lot of care or knowledge. After blooming, its stems turn woody, and you should remove them to encourage new growth that will bloom again. It also attracts pollinators, which is great for the entire wall.

Creeping phlox loves the sun and adapts easily to any type of soil. It will thrive if given enough light and doesn't need much more.

- Plant it at the soil level, not burying the stem, in well-draining soil.
- Water it regularly until established. During hot periods, water it more often.
- Fertilize it in early spring.
- Cut stems back after blooming to encourage more flowers to grow.

Snow-in-Summer

https://unsplash.com/photos/a-bunch-of-white-flowers-in-a-field-W1oAcJD848U

This flower gets its name from its appearance and the time of year at which it blooms. It blooms in early summertime, covering the ground with beautiful white flowers that look like snow.

This flower spreads easily, so if you're planting it in your living wall, it is recommended to contain it to where you want it using individual containers. To be certain to avoid spread, you may also cut off its stems right after flowering.

Snow-in-summer likes the sun and should be planted in the early spring. It will adapt to most soils if they are well-drained but might be more successful in sandy soil that is not rich in nutrients. It will tolerate short periods of drought.

- Sow seeds in a (very) well-draining soil.
- Water it sparsely.
- There is no need to fertilize this flower.
- Prune older blooms every year to keep them looking neat.

Trumpet Vine

https://pixabay.com/sv/photos/trumpetblomma-blomning-orange-1521462/

This flower is a showstopper! It has beautiful orange and burnt-orange tube-shaped flowers that really stand out against its dark green leaves. If you're a bird lover, then you'll probably want to make this a must on your living wall because trumpet vines attract hummingbirds! However, many gardeners wouldn't recommend growing this flower because it's a fast-growth one. It can easily take over other plants and grow up to forty feet in a single season! So, if you decide to plant it in your living wall in a container, you might have a better chance at keeping it under control. Pruning it often is recommended.

Trumpet vine should be planted in the spring or early fall. It likes sunlight and will produce the best flowers when it has at least half a day of light.

- Plant seeds in well-draining soil.
- Watering is not usually needed and should only be done if there are clear signs of wilting.
- No fertilizer is recommended due to its aggressive growth.
- Prune it regularly and pull out any new shoots you find.

Be careful if you decide to plant this flower, as every part of it is poisonous if ingested or if it touches your skin.

Wisteria

https://pixabay.com/es/photos/wisteria-glicina-flor-floreciente-5126106/

Even though it is a gorgeous vining flower, Wisteria is aggressive in its growth, much like the trumpet vine. They can easily crowd out other plants, and you shouldn't grow them near your home. Some varieties are non-invasive such as the Amethyst Falls Wisteria, so consider this type if you really want to plant it against a wall in your home.

Wisteria blooms lavender flowers in the spring and should be planted in early spring or fall. They take a long time to fully mature, so it is advised to buy established plants instead. They like the sun and fertile, moist soil.

- Plant established plants in well-draining soil.
- Apply mulch to retain moisture and prevent weeds.

- Water the plant if it hasn't rained that week.
- Prune it twice a year – in late winter and during the summer for a more controlled, neat-looking vine.

In the tables below, you'll find a summary of these flowers' requirements for easier comparison between them. They are divided into two tables: one for vining flowers, the other for cascading flowers.

Vining Flowers

Flower	Sun Exposure	Soil Type	Soil pH	Bloom	Perennial
Climbing Hydrangea	Partial shade	Loamy	Slightly Acidic	Spring, Summer	Yes
Climbing Rose	Full sun, Part sun	Loamy	Neutral	Late Spring to early Fall	Yes
Trumpet Vine	Full sun, Part sun	Any	Neutral to Acidic	Summer	Yes
Wisteria	Full sun, Part sun	Any	Slightly Acidic to Neutral	Spring	Yes

Cascading Flowers

Flower	Sun Exposure	Soil Type	Soil pH	Bloom	Perennial
Aurina	Full sun	Chalky, sandy, loamy	Neutral to Alkaline	Spring	Yes
Clematis	Full sun, Part sun	Loamy	Varies according to the variety chosen	Varies according to the variety chosen	Yes
Creeping Phlox	Full sun, Part sun	Any	Neutral	Mid-Spring, Summer	Yes
Snow-in-Summer	Full sun	Sandy	Neutral	Early summer	Yes

As you can see, the options are endless, and it's up to you and your creativity to turn your living wall into your favorite space. You can match colors or go with a less traditional route and use flowers that clash. Use a mix of sun-loving flowers on the top rows and place those that prefer shade on the lower rows. You can even go with only one type of flower if you want! It's your living wall; it's your time, effort, and patience, so you're the only one who can make these decisions. Turning your living wall into something you love will ensure you spend a lot of time taking care of it, not because you have to, but because you love it.

You may now be wondering how to take care of these plants, flowers, vegetables, or fruits. In the next chapter, we talk about how to control weeds, pests, and disease, so that you know what to do if any of these problems arise.

Chapter 10: Controlling Weeds, Diseases, and Pests

Making your own vertical garden or living wall is not all fun and games. The positive aspect is that you will end up with a breathtaking space that will help you relax and improve your life.

However, besides the care and patience, you have to give your vertically grown space, you also have to think about weeds, diseases, and pests. It's not the glamorous side of things, but it is a factor you have to deal with sooner or later, and I strongly recommend that you handle it as soon as possible.

Controlling weeds, diseases, and pests is not only an issue for in-ground gardeners. Soil, water, and other factors may lead to these problems, and you will need to think about how you want to solve these issues. As always, planning ahead will ensure you have the means and knowledge to get ahead of whatever problem you may face and eradicate it quickly.

You may think that using pesticides will solve all your problems, but they may not always be the solution you should be going for. What things should you consider when controlling weeds, diseases, and pests? What problems can arise, and how do you fix them? Let's dive into it.

What Contributes to Weeds, Diseases, and Pests?

Some of the things that may affect your plants and contribute to weeds, diseases, and pests are imbalanced soil, watering, and pesticides. That's right; sometimes, in trying to fight off the problem, you're only adding to it by using pesticides.

Insects like moths, butterflies, and other small insects like to chew on your damaged plants. You may find yellow spots on the leaves of your plants which indicate that tiny insects are around. Of course, you don't want insects eating away at your crops, but you may be creating another problem by eliminating this issue with pesticides. This is especially true when gardeners use a general insecticide, not knowing which insect is chewing their plants. This may cause another problem because a general insecticide will also kill off the insects that may be beneficial to your plants. You need to understand that harmful insects are present because of a damaged plant; they don't feed off healthy ones. In other words, they are not the root cause of the problem. They are a symptom of it, and you should be addressing the actual cause by looking into why your plant is damaged.

If your plants have a disease, then it may be biotic or abiotic. Like the name indicates, biotic diseases are caused by living organisms and abiotic by non-living agents like herbicides, pollution, or nutrients. Once again, these diseases may appear due to an imbalance in the soil, which will be more likely to get attacked by insects. There are certain insects like leafhoppers that may also spread diseases when feeding. But we know there is a root problem that needs to be addressed first: soil, water, plant damage. These are most likely to be the causes of weeds, diseases, and pests.

What Issues Should You Pay Attention To?

Issues in a living wall or vertical garden are similar to general issues any gardener finds in their garden. The main difference is that a vertical garden is likely to have fewer diseases and pests because the soil used is controlled. Using drip irrigation systems will also help with root rot and overwatering problems because it's a slow, precise system. But this doesn't mean that issues won't appear, so paying attention to your plants and living wall is worth it.

In vertical gardens or living walls, the most common issues are over-or-underwatering, sunlight/shade, imbalance of soil, and plant diseases. It is important to identify the issue quickly before your entire wall or garden is affected.

Watering Needs

Even though it's easy to find out the watering needs of a plant, most gardeners tend to water their plants a little too heavily, which leads to all sorts of problems. Making sure you do not overwater your plants is Rule Number One of keeping a beautiful, healthy vertical garden or living wall.

You can try using an automated drip irrigation system so that the task is automated or double-check every time to see if the soil is ready for more watering before you do it. Stick to your plant's schedule, and you should be fine.

A sign that you may be overwatering your plants is if the leaves wilt or turn yellow. You may also see mold on top of the soil, or the stem may feel soft to the touch. If these signs are occurring, do not panic; just stop watering your plant for a few days. Let the plant regain its energy, and make sure the soil is fully dry before you start watering it again. You may also re-pot the entire plant, but if you let it breathe and your space has good air circulation, the plant will have a fighting chance.

If you're not overwatering, you may be underwatering your plants. Even though this is less common, it sometimes happens among new gardeners. The signs of underwatering are different from overwatering because the plants won't be getting the nutrients they need. They may experience slow growth, their leaves' edges may be turning brown and start to curl, they won't have any blossoms, and their stems will be brittle and crisp. Underwatering is just as bad as overwatering. You will still be harming your plants, so make sure you follow a strict watering schedule and respect your plants' needs.

Sunlight vs. Shade

Most plants need light to help them grow, so you have to give them that light. Once again, each plant is different and will have slightly different needs. Getting too little or too much light will result in an unhealthy-looking vertical garden or living wall.

Respect the instructions on how to handle your plant. If a plant requires 6-8 hours of light daily and your chosen location doesn't allow for this, then you need to move it somewhere else or avoid buying that plant in the first place. It's just a headache you want to avoid.

If your plants' leaves are falling off or growing lanky, this is a sign of an unhealthy plant. This plant needs more light. If the leaves are crunchy or you find scorched spots on them, then your plant is probably receiving too much light.

Light exposure is important for your plants, and it is something you can fix. However, it would be simpler if you think about this aspect before buying a certain type of plant that isn't suitable for the location you have in mind for it.

Imbalanced Soil

In Chapter 3, we talk about the importance of soil mixtures, types, and pH levels. Every plant is different and may need adjustments, and if you're not providing these, your plants will not flourish. For example, soil that is not well-draining affects the plants' roots, stems, and leaves. It will harm your plants, and you won't even be able to see that at first.

Check drainage before planting by watering your soil and seeing if there's water escaping your container. You don't want to find it all because that would imply your plant won't be getting enough nutrients, but there needs to be *some* drainage. Checking before planting is the easiest way to avoid problems in the future.

Pests and Plant Diseases

Even though there is a lower risk because of controlled soil, water systems, and the structure being off the ground, vertical gardens may still suffer from pests and diseases. These are more difficult to solve than overwatering, for example, but there are solutions available. Some of them may even be found in your pantry.

If you find out your vertical structure has a pest or disease problem, here's how you can deal with that issue.

How to Control or Deal with these Problems:

The first and obvious answer to this is prevention. Prevention is an easier way to get healthy, tasty crops than solving your problems later on. Healthy plants are not likely to get diseases or pests. By ensuring your soil is the right mix for your plants, using the right compost and mulch, removing old leaves, weeds, and following the instructions given for your specific plant, you are taking the necessary steps to prevent pests and disease from appearing.

Even rotating plants will help with prevention. Even if it seems like it will take longer to get your vertical garden set up, it will help you in the long run. If you still encounter a problem even after having done this, this is how you should handle it:

- **Investigate the Situation**

You do not want to act before identifying which pest or disease is attacking your plant, so investigate first. Give yourself time to find the root cause of the problem so that your solution will be effective and the least dangerous to your plant.

- **Give It Time**

Give your plant time to fix the problem on its own. If not seriously damaged, your plant or other plants nearby may help you fix the problem themselves. Nature is just that incredible, and if you allow it some time, maybe you won't have to take any actions. Some insects, for example, may come to the rescue and eat the disease away. Other plants may overtake the sickly ones so that you just have to remove the damaged ones. Give it time.

- **A Kind Solution**

If you must take matters into your own hands, go with the solution that is kind to the environment, to your plants, and to you. There are so many ways around it that you really don't have to go running for the chemical pesticides to solve your problems. Mulching helps with weeds, for example. You can even buy beneficial bugs at a store. The goal is not to reach for a chemical pesticide immediately but to think before you act.

With that said, sometimes, there *is* a need for a pesticide. However, the solution is to make your own, so you are fully aware of what's in it. You will find below three DIY pesticides that are kind to the environment.

1. Neem Oil

This oil is a great option when dealing with pests and diseases in plants. It'll affect chewing insects but not pollinators, which your plants always need. You can use it as a spray or add it directly to the soil when you have young plants – the oil will seep through the soil, the plants will absorb it, and once insects chew on them, they will die off. To make it into a spray, this is what you will need:

- 2 teaspoons of neem oil
- 1 teaspoon of liquid soap
- 8.5 ounces of water

Mix in the three ingredients, pour them into a spray bottle and shake it well. Then spray the mixture onto the leaves (top and bottom), ensuring they are well soaked in the product. Spray them early morning or in the evening when they are not facing direct sunlight.

This mixture will help with mealybugs, whiteflies, aphids, and even root rot and black spots.

2. Baking Soda

Baking soda is known for its dozens of uses around the house, so it's no surprise that it can also help you in the garden. This ingredient is present in most households and is an effective one in treating black spots. This is what you'll need:

- 4 teaspoons of baking soda
- 1 teaspoon of mild liquid soap
- 10 oz of water

Mix the three ingredients well, pour them into a spray bottle, and shake it well. Then spray the mixture onto the leaves, making sure you cover both sides. Continue shaking the spray so that it doesn't separate. Ensure you cover the entire plant, including shoots and new leaves, even if it doesn't seem like they're infected. This mixture will help with black-spot and white mildew.

3. Used Coffee Grounds and Crushed Eggshells

This DIY is not much of a DIY as it is just two ingredients that you should add to your plants that will create a barrier for insects. Used coffee grounds and crushed eggshells will deter some insects from attacking your plants, and these two household items can be found in any home. Plus, it's almost as if you're composting or recycling, so bonus points for that!

Used coffee grounds – these have a much lower pH, so they're better to mix in with the soil. You can sprinkle some on top of the soil or mix them lightly into the soil. Coffee grounds stop ants and other chewing insects from coming onto your plants.

Crushed eggshells – this household ingredient is high in calcium carbonate, which deters slugs and snails from climbing your plants. Any other ingredients also high in calcium carbonate would help, but crushed eggshells are sharp, which is another advantage to using them.

Whether they are simple or complex, dealing with issues in your vertical garden or living wall is daunting for many first-time gardeners, so you're not alone in feeling that way. Use the above methods and procedures to help you solve your gardening issues, and you will soon find your plants looking happy and healthy again. The most important step is the first one, to have control.

If you're observant, you will detect a problem quickly and be able to fix it just as quickly.

You're right at the end of your journey into becoming a vertical garden or living wall connoisseur; you're ready to get your hands dirty! Let's look at a checklist of everything you'll need from the start of your journey until the end – well, maybe until the middle; this book won't give you recipes to teach you what to do with your fruits and vegetables after you harvest them.

Chapter 11: Your Vertical Gardening Checklist

This chapter will look at a final checklist of everything you need for a vertical garden or living wall. This is it; you're ready to start on your path to becoming a vertical gardener. You have studied and learned how to start this journey from scratch. It's been a long, daunting road, full of information and tips on making this first time a successful one, but you should be confident that you have the tools you need to make it on your own.

If you've forgotten what steps are the most important to consider when starting your vertical garden or living wall, do not worry. What you'll find below is a detailed list of these steps that will put you on the right path and lead you to the finish line. Use the checklist at the end of the chapter to make sure you haven't forgotten anything, and tick off each step as you go along.

Steps to Take for Your Vertical Garden or Living Wall

Which Structure to Choose?

You know by now that the first step is to decide if you want a vertical garden or living wall and which type of support you'll choose for your base. Will you go for a trellis or a more DIY approach? The type of vertical structure you choose will be important for finding out what types of plants you can grow. Moreover, deciding on the type of support early on will make it easier to design it the way you want.

Do you want a luscious green wall or some pops of color peeking through by adding flowers? Do you want a tiered system so you can easily install a drip irrigation system? Or maybe you prefer the contrast between nature and concrete and want to plant your green plants and flowers in cinder blocks. Or you can go for a simple, farmhouse style with mason jars and a wood plank right in your kitchen for easy reach.

Thinking ahead allows you to plan the design of your vertical garden or living wall. This is especially important if you're trying to catch people's attention by creating intricate shapes and details on your wall. Certain designs will allow a hydroponic system to be installed, and others won't. So planning ahead will give you the flexibility to choose and change your mind before anything's done.

Materials and Hardware

You need to think about which materials you'll need to add to your wall or the structure you may be building. You may need wood to build a few boxes or a ladder. You may need hooks to hang your containers from. You will most likely need to waterproof your wall with paint, plastic, or other materials to ensure that it doesn't get damaged by the humidity.

Getting the materials all at once will save you the headache of going back and forth to the store. Decide on the support system you want, write a list of all the materials and hardware you'll need to build it or add onto it, and you're set for a perfect start.

Location

The wall or location you choose for your vertical structure is important because of the light that reaches it, the air circulation it has, and ultimately, the plants you will be able to pick. If you have certain types of plants in mind, then you might have to be more flexible with the location you choose for your vertical garden or living wall. However, if you're set on a spot, you need to be more flexible with your choice of plants. This is especially true for those living in small apartments with a tiny balcony or a small amount of available space. You want to make sure to choose somewhere you'll love having a green wall, but also somewhere where it works.

Getting to know the placement of your vertical structure before choosing your plants will set you on the right track for growing healthy, lush plants.

Which Plants to Pick

Having figured out where your vertical garden or living wall will be set up is key to selecting your plants correctly. You'll know how many hours of light you have during the day or if you need strong plants that can withstand wind.

Picking plants may seem daunting, but it can be made simpler by answering the question: will you want them to be edible or not? If yes, you should focus on vegetables and fruits that you can grow in the same vertical garden. But, if you answer no, then it's all about the plants and flowers you love that are also suited for the space you've selected.

Different Soils for Plants' Specifications

The soil is the home of every plant. Sticking to your plants' specifications is key for a good start when taking care of them. If a plant needs clay soil and you put it in a loamy one, your plant won't thrive. The same goes for drainage issues: if your soil is not adapted to your plants' needs, you'll be facing root rot, diseases, and unhealthy plants.

It's important to read about your plants to find the best soil match for each one of them. Refer to Chapter 2 for a more detailed and thorough look into the soil types and specifications if you need help with this.

Watering Method

Do you have time to water your plants a few times a week? Will you stop yourself from overwatering them? Do you have the budget to incorporate an automated irrigation system into your vertical structure? These are questions that will help you decide which watering method you should use for your vertical garden or living wall.

Contrary to popular belief, living walls can be watered manually. They don't all need a sophisticated hydroponic system to grow well and be healthy. It may take you more time to water them manually, but it will be easier on your pockets.

The watering system you choose will directly affect your vertical garden or living wall, so choose wisely and take your time to reflect on what works best for you. Look again at Chapters 2 and 5 if you want more information on irrigation systems and how to make your own.

Fertilizers

Thinking about the soil and water won't be enough to help your plants grow healthy but considering your fertilizer options will help the process. Fertilizers may be added at the moment of planting and during the growth period. Sometimes, if the soil drains a little too well, nutrients won't be absorbed by the plants. Adding fertilizers and mulching will help your plants tremendously.

Read about your plant's specifications to discover which nutrients they need the most and make sure they get them. You should think about whether you want to add chemicals to your plants or not. If you don't want to add chemicals, think of ways to use organic matter or natural solutions to give your plants what they need.

Environmentally Friendly DIYs

Thinking ahead of the potential problems that may arise is intelligent because you'll be ready to solve them if they happen. Considering your options to control weeds, pests, and diseases before you find them will give you a better chance of helping your plants survive. The easiest route is to buy a pesticide from the store, but as you may remember, in Chapter 10, we talked about how you can fix different issues with nonchemical homemade products, most of which are in your pantry.

It is smart to be prepared because even if you do not need to spray your plants down with some pesticide, you will feel confident that you haven't overlooked anything and are ready for whatever may come.

Garden Tools

You will need gardening tools to work on your vertical gardening when harvesting and pruning, and taking care of your plants in general. Getting them right at the start will ensure you have everything you may need before you need it. This way, you won't have to waste valuable time getting them later.

Eventually, you will most likely need a few tools, so consider buying pruning shears, a garden fork and a trowel, a spade, gloves, loppers, a watering can (if applicable,) and maybe a hoe and a rake if you have a large garden space. Getting the tools right from the start will help the process along.

To recap, this is the final vertical gardening checklist:

- Vertical structure
- Materials and hardware
- Location
- Which plants to pick
- Different soils for plants' specifications

- Watering method
- Fertilizers
- Environmentally friendly DIYs
- Garden tools

Once you've ticked off each step, you'll know you're ready to start. I know it has been a long road, but you are now ready for whatever may come. With the right tools and knowledge, your plants will be beautiful and healthy, and you'll be able to enjoy them soon. In the next and final chapter, we'll discuss the final precautions and considerations one should make before going into vertical gardening.

Chapter 12: Final Precautions and Considerations

Growing your own garden without compromising floor space is the only option for many homeowners. Vertical gardens and living walls hit the mark by taking up little space and giving new gardeners the option of having their own green paradise on their tiny balcony or small backyard or even inside their home.

Creating a living wall will also allow you to be more creative and hands-on throughout the entire process. However, this may not be for everyone, and there are many things to consider before diving into this new world. Obviously, you want to make the best decision for you, your budget, and even your free time, so having a clear goal and detailed plan is paramount for a successful vertical garden. In this chapter, we'll look at the pros and cons of having your own vertical garden or living wall, which will hopefully help you make the final decision.

Pros and Cons to Consider

Pros

Space Saver

Not everyone has a lot of empty space in their home or garden to plant their favorite crops; therefore, a vertical garden or living wall will provide you with the same option while being a space saver. The fact that these gardens grow up (and down) and not out allows you to grow up to five times more than traditional horizontal gardening, so you only need enough height to grow your favorite plants.

An Art Installation

Besides having a practical side, a vertical garden or living wall can be absolutely stunning, making it seem almost like an art installation rather than just a garden. If you plan which types of plants and the colors you'll mix and match, your vertical structure will say a lot more than "I'm here to feed you." A tall, lush green wall welcomes any customer or guest into space in the best way possible.

Creativity

Creating your own vertical garden or living wall will make you use your creativity. That is the beauty of these gardens as well. If this is a passion project and you're a creative person, you'll soon realize you can be very artistic with this space. You can plan which materials, plants, and colors you want to add to your vertical structure. You may even need to be creative when choosing which structure to utilize.

More Variety

Because the plants outlined in this book grow upwards, you may grow a wide variety of plants that you otherwise wouldn't be able to. Having a vertical structure with individual pockets will allow you to grow many varieties of plants or vegetables and herbs that would take up a large amount of space in a more traditional garden.

Privacy

Besides being aesthetically pleasing, vertical gardens and living walls may also help you by giving you some privacy or creating a cover from a busy road or nearby neighbors. It's a natural and beautiful way to add a little more intimacy to your balcony or yard without breaking the bank or creating an eyesore for your neighbors.

Easier for Beginners

A vertical garden or living wall is an easier option for beginners. The amount of care the plants will need is much less when compared to traditional gardening methods. Some vertical gardens or living walls do not even use soil, so the potential problems that arise with most crops wouldn't be a problem here. This is a smart and easy choice for a beginner.

Mobility

Due to modular containers and, most likely, smaller containers, mobility is one of the biggest pros of vertical gardens and living walls. You'll be able to move things around and switch them up as needed. Moreover, while maintaining them, you won't have to bend over for hours or hurt your knees in the process because everything is vertical. This is a major factor to consider, especially when one reaches a certain age.

No Clutter

Having potted plants is great, but when you have various vases and containers scattered all over the place, it can create a very messy, cluttered look. Having a vertical structure with all your pots or containers on a single wall will make the place look neater. In this case, you can even have different containers because once your plants grow and start hanging down, you won't see them anyway.

Noise-Reducing

A vertical garden and living wall can help with your concentration and productivity. They act as noise-reducing barriers and would make a great addition to an open-plan office space or even an apartment located in a busy area. Block out the sound of traffic by installing your own green wall.

Stress Relief

These vertical structures will positively affect your health, and one of the ways they can do that is by acting as a stress reliever. Studies conducted by Alan Ewert and Yun Chang have shown that being surrounded by a green, natural environment lowers your heart rate, blood pressure, and general stress in a matter of minutes. In a world where everything rushes by at 100 miles a minute, having something that helps you calm down during the day is beneficial.

Recycling

Another positive aspect of creating your vertical garden or living wall is the potential for recycling. If making it yourself, you'll be able to reuse materials you have lying around your home, such as plastic water bottles or even containers you no longer need. You'll be contributing to a greener world not just literally but also through the choices of materials and tools you use.

Cons

Not Enough Space for Roots

By having plants too close to each other or in smaller containers, your plant's roots won't have a lot of space to grow. This need not be a huge issue, but it will most likely translate into smaller crops. In a traditional garden, you leave more space between crops for proper growth, and roots have all the space they need to grow.

Dry Out

The problem with vertical gardens or living walls is that the top plants may dry out quicker than they normally would had they been planted in the ground. Due to the weather, airflow, and sunlight, plants on top rows may dry out. A solution for this is to move your plants occasionally.

Sun Blockers

Just as the top plants might fry out, they may also block other plants from getting sunlight. Because they'll grow and cascade over the edges of their containers, the top rows of plants may overshadow the ones underneath them, blocking any light from reaching them. The solution to this is the same as the previous one; rotate your crops regularly. Getting modular containers is the key to streamlining this process.

Expensive

Even though there are a few hacks, tips, and tricks you can use to make your own vertical structure, it can still be quite expensive. If you add up the cost of materials, soil, irrigation systems, plants, and tools you'll need in the long run, this project can become quite expensive. This can be helped with some careful planning before you purchase any items. Look for cheaper options and reusing materials. However, if you decide to buy a ready-made vertical structure, it can be quite pricey.

Messy

Unfortunately, this has to be said: vertical gardens and living walls can be really messy. Dirt may fall off from containers, water splashes everywhere, and leaves fall. All of these things are normal and will happen. This won't be a big deal in a traditional garden, but when growing against a wall on a balcony, you may have to constantly clean your floor. A tray at the bottom of the structure will help but will not entirely prevent it from happening.

Humidity

Another problem is caused by having water near or against a wall. If not properly prepared and insulated, humidity and mold will appear and may damage your wall. This is not ideal, and you don't want to have to deal with mold later on. So make sure you prepare your wall correctly and check on it from time to time to detect any problems early on.

More Maintenance

Even though you won't have to deal with as many weeds or certain issues that are more common in traditional gardens, there is substantial maintenance to keep up with when it comes to vertical gardens and living walls. Plants living in these containers will need constant care. They will need regular pruning and trimming, careful and calculated addition of nutrients, and even adjusted watering methods. You will also need to be more vigilant. But, because it won't be a large structure, you won't have to spend all your free time taking care of it.

No Support for Heavier Crops

The most common vertical gardens won't be sturdy enough for certain heavy crops like melons and squashes, even if they can grow vertically. Making sure you have the right support for whatever you're growing is important to avoid damage when the plants start fruiting.

These are the pros and cons in a simple, easy to remember list:

Pros	Cons
Space saver	Not enough root space
An art installation	Dry out
Creativity	Sun blockers
Grow more variety	Expensive
Privacy	Messy
Easier for beginners	Humidity
Mobility	More maintenance
No clutter	No support for heavier crops
Noise-reduction	
Stress relief	
Recycling	

These are the main pros and cons of building a vertical garden or living wall, but another big question that you should ask yourself is, "Is this sustainable?"

Is a Vertical Garden or Living Wall Sustainable?

When thinking about this question, you can think of two things: is this sustainable for you? And is this a sustainable, environmentally friendly structure?

For starters, a green wall is a new, modern way of achieving sustainability in buildings where environmentally friendly foundations were not considered at the time of building. A green wall may be added later to the bland, concrete building and provide many health benefits for its tenants and owners. Moreover, installing a green wall in your business may translate into more sales and draw people's attention. This may lead to financial growth, which is positive for any business, but is it sustainable? Will you choose to have a green wall because of its benefits if, in the end, it could cause more problems?

Is a green wall sustainable for you? Is the time and effort you have to allot to it sustainable in the long term? Everyone is enamored with the idea of a green wall these days, but many don't consider its risks. This is a structure that requires time, effort, money, and attention. If you're not capable of giving it the right amount of these things, this is not a sustainable idea for you, and you should re-consider it.

Reflecting on whether building it yourself or buying a ready-made vertical structure is about more than that initial effort and time it'll take you to get it up and running. This is a commitment, maybe not for life but for a long time, that should be taken seriously, and if you don't think you're ready for it, you should assess those feelings.

However, if you're excited about this new step but maybe feeling a little nervous, that is normal. It's like when you start a new job or move to a new city, it may be nerve-wracking at first, but you can do it! With the right guidelines and help, you can achieve anything you put your mind to! Your very own vertical garden or living wall is just a few steps away, and you should be excited for this new journey you're about to embark on. It's going to be a fun one!

Conclusion

We hope this book has been useful to you. This started as a vertical gardening beginner's guide to growing fruit, vegetables, herbs, or flowers on a vertical structure. However, you should feel more confident than a beginner by now. You have learned the basics of vertical gardening, including how to plant crops and plants, so your journey should feel easier.

Good luck with creating your first vertical garden or living wall - you can do this!

Here's another book by Dion Rosser that you might like

DION ROSSER

COMPOSTING

The Ultimate Guide to Creating Your Own Organic Compost in Your Backyard and Using It for Organic Gardening to Create a More Self-Sufficient Garden

References

3 signs your green wall is in trouble [and what to do about it]. (n.d.). Retrieved from Growupgreenwalls.com website: https://growupgreenwalls.com/blogs/growupdates/3-signs-your-green-wall-is-in-trouble-and-what-to-do-about-it

Albert, S. (2015, June 8). 10 natural, organic steps to control garden pests and diseases. Retrieved from Harvesttotable.com website: https://harvesttotable.com/10-natural-organic-steps-to-control-garden-pests-and-diseases/

Amber. (2018, December 29). The 15 best perennials for A vertical garden - garden tabs. Retrieved from Gardentabs.com website: https://gardentabs.com/best-perennials-vertical-garden/

Andrychowicz, A. (2019, March 25). The amazing benefits of vertical gardening. Retrieved from Getbusygardening.com website: https://getbusygardening.com/vertical-gardening-benefits

Aurinia saxatilis (Basket-of-Gold). (n.d.). Retrieved from Gardenia.net website: https://www.gardenia.net/plant/aurinia-saxatilis-basket-of-gold

BBC Gardeners' World Magazine. (2019, July 5). Plants for a living wall. Retrieved from Gardenersworld.com website: https://www.gardenersworld.com/plants/plants-for-a-living-wall/

Benefits of outdoor living green walls and vertical gardens. (2017, October 19). Retrieved from Biotecture.uk.com website: https://www.biotecture.uk.com/benefits/benefits-of-exterior-living-walls/

Best plants for vertical gardens. (2016, May 4). Retrieved from Balconygardenweb.com website: https://balconygardenweb.com/best-plants-for-vertical-garden-vertical-garden-plants/

Best Vining fruits and vegetables for vertical gardens. (n.d.). Retrieved from Davesgarden.com website: https://davesgarden.com/guides/articles/best-vining-fruits-and-vegetables-for-vertical-gardens

Brougham, R. (2018, February 12). 14 Inspiring DIY Flower Walls. Retrieved from Familyhandyman.com website: https://www.familyhandyman.com/list/14-inspiring-diy-flower-walls/

Dian. (2019, July 10). Getting started vertical gardening: Tools you'll need. Retrieved from Dianfarmer.com website: https://dianfarmer.com/getting-started-vertical-gardening-tools-youll-need/

Drip Irrigation for Living Walls. (2018, March 29). Retrieved from Plantsonwalls.com website: https://www.plantsonwalls.com/guides/drip-irrigation-living-walls/

Dyer, M. H. (2018, July 10). The upsides and downsides of vertical gardening. Retrieved from Gardeningknowhow.com website: https://blog.gardeningknowhow.com/gardening-pros-cons/vertical-gardening-pros-and-cons-2/

Editors, R. S. (2015, July 1). Everything you need to know to grow your own vertical garden. Retrieved from Realsimple.com website: https://www.realsimple.com/home-organizing/gardening/how-to-make-a-vertical-garden

Garden Design Magazine. (2015, July 14). 12 garden tools to buy - essentials for beginners - garden design. Retrieved from Gardendesign.com website: https://www.gardendesign.com/how-to/tools.html

Home Improvement Pages Australia. (n.d.). Choosing irrigation systems for vertical gardens. Retrieved from Com.au website: https://hipages.com.au/article/choosing_irrigation_systems_for_vertical_gardens

Horticulture Landscaping: Vertical Gardening. (n.d.). Retrieved from Tnau.ac.in website: https://agritech.tnau.ac.in/horticulture/horti_Landscaping_vertical%20gardening.html

How to start a vertical garden today. (2018, March 6). Retrieved from Growingorganic.com website: https://growingorganic.com/diy-guide/how-to-start-a-vertical-garden/

Justin. (2019, February 1). Vertical gardening pros and cons - garden tabs. Retrieved from Gardentabs.com website: https://gardentabs.com/pros-cons/

Kinetic Design-http://www. kinetic. co. (n.d.). How to grow herbs in A vertical garden. Retrieved from Com.au website: https://www.baileysfertiliser.com.au/gardening-blog/guide-to-growing-herbs-in-a-vertical-garden

Lafreniere, A. (2019, December 11). Living wall pest control. Retrieved from Planthardware.com website: https://planthardware.com/living-wall-pest-control/

Levin, A. (2017, July 18). How to design and install a living wall. Retrieved from Fesmag.com website: https://fesmag.com/topics/trends/14894-how-to-design-and-install-a-living-wall

Living Wall Systems. (n.d.). Retrieved from Ansgroupglobal.com website: https://www.ansgroupglobal.com/living-wall

Lowin, R., & SanSone, A. E. (2018, March 3). 35 DIY vertical garden ideas to show off your green thumb. Retrieved from Countryliving.com website: https://www.countryliving.com/gardening/garden-ideas/how-to/g1274/how-to-plant-a-vertical-garden

Magyar, C. (2020, April 17). 10 fruits and veggies to grow vertically for epic yields in tiny spaces. Retrieved from Ruralsprout.com website: https://www.ruralsprout.com/grow-food-vertically/

Martin, K. (2021, February 12). 12 climbing fruit plants. Retrieved from Urbangardengal.com website: https://www.urbangardengal.com/climbing-fruit-plants/

Metson, E. (2019, August 28). Are living walls worth creating over other sustainable options? Retrieved from Biofriendlyplanet.com website: https://biofriendlyplanet.com/green-alternatives/sustainable/are-living-walls-worth-creating-over-other-sustainable-options/

Natasha. (2016, January 11). 12 ideas which materials to use to make A vertical garden. Retrieved from Fantasticviewpoint.com website: http://www.fantasticviewpoint.com/12-ideas-materials-use-make-vertical-garden/

Natural Pest & Weed Control. (n.d.). Retrieved from Savingwater.org website: https://www.savingwater.org/lawn-garden/natural-pest-weed-control/

Natural remedies for pest, disease, and weed control. (2020). Elsevier.

Nichols, M. R. (2018, March 1). Green walls are great, but they need to work efficiently. Retrieved from Inhabitat.com website: https://inhabitat.com/green-walls-are-great-but-they-need-to-work-efficiently/

Old Farmer's Almanac. (n.d.). Growing Guides. Retrieved from Almanac.com website: https://www.almanac.com/gardening/growing-guides

Osmond, C. (n.d.). 56 of the best vertical gardening ideas: #27 is gorgeous! Retrieved from Backyardboss.net website: https://www.backyardboss.net/best-vertical-gardening-ideas

Planting guide. (2018, May 18). Retrieved from Livewall.com website: https://livewall.com/plant-selection/planting-guide/

Plants & Flowers. (n.d.). Retrieved from Thespruce.com website: https://www.thespruce.com/plants-and-flowers-5092674

Poindexter, J. (2018, April 17). How to start a DIY vertical garden (and 7 ideas you should try). Retrieved from Morningchores.com website: https://morningchores.com/vertical-garden/

Pot, S. (2018, August 21). What is the best soil for fruit trees? Retrieved from Springpot.com website: https://www.springpot.com/best-soil-for-fruit-trees/

Pros and cons of vertical gardens. (2013, April 10). Retrieved from Easyverticalgardening.com website: https://easyverticalgardening.com/types-of-vertical-gardens/pros-and-cons-of-vertical-gardens/

Search, plants - BBC gardeners' world magazine. (n.d.). Retrieved from Gardenersworld.com website: https://www.gardenersworld.com/search/plants/

Smith, A., & Clapp, L. (2021, March 24). How to make a living wall – an easy step by step to DIY your own living wall system. Retrieved from Realhomes.com website: https://www.realhomes.com/advice/how-to-create-a-living-wall

Sood, G. (2019, April 11). Indoor vertical garden: How to grow & things to consider. Retrieved from Homecrux.com website: https://www.homecrux.com/indoor-vertical-garden/120830/

The Daily Gardener. (2020, July 27). 7 easy steps to construct a perfect vertical garden. Retrieved from Thedailygardener.com website: https://www.thedailygardener.com/construct-vertical-garden

The planter box approach to green walls. (2018, October 5). Retrieved from Com.au website: https://www.tensile.com.au/the-planter-box-approach-to-green-walls/

The pros and cons of a living wall. (n.d.). Retrieved from Calibre-furniture.co.uk website: https://www.calibre-furniture.co.uk/blog/the-pros-and-cons-of-a-living-wall

Tilley, N. (2007, July 13). Growing A vertical vegetable garden. Retrieved from Gardeningknowhow.com website: https://www.gardeningknowhow.com/edible/vegetables/vgen/growing-a-vertical-vegetable-garden.htm

Tirelli, G. (2019, April 2). Top 10 benefits of living green walls or vertical. Retrieved from Ecobnb.com website: https://ecobnb.com/blog/2019/04/living-green-walls-benefits/

TOP 10 Plants for Vertical Garden. (2017, June 6). Retrieved from Nurserylive.com website: https://wiki.nurserylive.com/t/top-10-plants-for-vertical-garden/2172

Ultimate Guide to Living Green Walls. (n.d.). Retrieved from Ambius.com website: https://www.ambius.com/green-walls/ultimate-guide-to-living-green-walls/

Vertical goodness: 10 DIY living walls kits for green living. (2017, August 8). Retrieved from Decoist.com website: https://www.decoist.com/diy-living-walls-kits/

What Are Vertical Gardens? (n.d.). Retrieved from Ambius.com website: https://www.ambius.com/green-walls/what-are-vertical-gardens

What foods can I grow in a vertical garden? (2018, August 14). Retrieved from Livewall.com website: https://livewall.com/faq-items/what-foods-can-i-grow-in-a-vertical-garden/

What Herbs grow best in a vertical garden? (2019, February 8). Retrieved from Easyverticalgardening.com website: https://easyverticalgardening.com/what-herbs-grow-best-in-a-vertical-garden/

Ewert, A., & Chang, Y. (2018). Levels of nature and stress response. *Behavioral Sciences, 8*(5). doi:10.3390/bs8050049

Printed in Great Britain
by Amazon